MAKE AMERICA STRONGER TOGETHER AGAIN

Make America Stronger Together Again

Looking Beyond America's Most Vitriolic Election

Gregory T. Christensen

American Blueprint Publishing

Copyright © 2018 by Gregory T. Christensen

All rights reserved. No part of this publication may be reproduced, distributed, or transmitted in any form or by any means, including photocopying, recording, or other electronic or mechanical methods, without the prior written permission of the publisher, except in the case of brief quotations embodied in critical reviews and certain other noncommercial uses permitted by copyright law. For permission requests, contact the publisher at info@americanblueprint.org

American Blueprint Publishing
Palm Springs, California
www.MastaBook.com
orders@americanblueprint.org

Ordering Information:
Quantity sales. Special discounts are available on quantity purchases by academic institutions, associations, and others.
Orders by U.S. trade bookstores and wholesalers. Please contact Ingram Distribution:
Ingram Content Group LLC
One Ingram Blvd.
La Vergne, TN 37086
Retail Stores (in USA) – 1 (800) 937-8000
Retail Stores (Outside USA) – 1 (615) 793-5000, ext. 27652

Library of Congress Control Number (LCCN): 2018905829

First Edition: July 2018

ISBNs: 978-1-7323608-0-8 (paperback), 978-1-7323608-1-5 (ebook)

Printed in the United States of America

LSC-C

10 9 8 7 6 5 4 3 2 1

For Ann, Deirdre, Don and Lorraine, Katie and David Godino, my role models Bill and Hillary Clinton, my mentor Wendell Vaughn, and everyone who continues to pick up the torch and keep fighting for America. Ours is a story less than half written. Let's write the next chapter together!

Contents

Introduction   1

PART ONE: LOOKING BACK

Chapter One: Hillary Rodham Clinton   7

Chapter Two: Donald J. Trump   19

Chapter Three: Democratic Primary – The Race for Iowa, the "Damn Emails", and History Made!   29

Chapter Four: Republican Primary - Low Energy Jeb, Lyin' Ted, and Little Marco   47

Chapter Five: The Presidential Campaign from Hell   63

Chapter Six: The October Surprise – A Basket of Deplorables On a Bus   85

Chapter Seven: Comey and the Investigation That Never Was   99

Chapter Eight: Election Night   113

PART TWO: MOVING FORWARD

Chapter Nine: The Morning After — 123

Chapter Ten: One Term – Four Years – 1461 Days — 135

Chapter Eleven: The Bankruptcy of an American Presidency – Restructuring the Country — 153

Chapter Twelve: Country First, Experienced Leadership — 179

Chapter Thirteen: Change We Can Believe In — 193

Chapter Fourteen: Believe in America — 201

Chapter Fifteen: Forward — 211

Chapter Sixteen: Tomorrow — 239

Afterward — 245

Acknowledgements — 249

About the Author — 253

Credits — 255

Introduction

It's all a horrifying, insidious nightmare. I know I'll wake up and find that: We are the United States. We are the most respected, prosperous, shining example of freedom ever. We are the country that stands together, a beacon of hope to the world. Instead, I wake up and discover we aren't. We aren't? We're different, we've changed, or maybe something else has taken place, something sinister – like an outright theft of America's presidency. "What happened?" I think to myself.

Each morning I wake to find an America in turmoil – a broken country, divided across obfuscated partisan lines. The distance between us seems to grow each day as new exchanges between politicians and their base conflict with opponents across the aisle. This distance has fractured the foundation of our nation's values, led to a kakistocracy, and pitted brother against brother. We've lost faith in each other and lost confidence in our political process. We've lost trust in our leaders and lost credibility on the global stage. "What happened?" I scream, realizing my nightmare is our new reality.

Americans used to find congeniality with those of opposing political perspectives. We used to talk about our differences on

Introduction

issues. Now it's almost impossible to discuss anything without first disclosing whom we voted for or what side we're on. Are you a Clinton supporter or a Trump defender? Do you prioritize values or care more about political wins?

Donald Trump's presidential campaign was quick to regenerate a Reagan era campaign slogan – Make America Great Again – that rapidly became the platitude of choice for his candidacy. While the country was left wondering when America was last great, Hillary Clinton and the Democrats pushed a more unified message – Stronger Together. Neither candidate was overwhelmingly liked outside of his or her core base of support, but their campaign slogans and aligned rhetoric solidified support for both. As the weeks careened toward Election Night, numerous scandals decelerated the political momentum of each campaign drawing one-time supporters to question their candidate's character. When the final votes were cast, the result caught us off guard. Given all that had happened before it – given all that we had been through as a country – the result was more than just unexpected, it was infuriating.

Scholars suggest that events like Pearl Harbor are the turning points that trigger related events to occur down the road. America has seen a number of these so-called "lynchpins" cause domestic and international chain reactions from the Boston Tea Party to the September 11th terror attacks. After each, America responded in a way that changed the course of history and made a profound impact on the world. November 8th, 2016, became our newest lynchpin. Reminiscent of a Rube Goldberg machine from our nightmares, Donald Trump ascended into the White House, activating a deluge of political consequences across our country. Bedrock government organizations were handed over to political

Introduction

neophytes, ethical nonpartisan public servants were ejected from their posts and replaced with sycophants, and the election of an unprepared political maverick spurred federal investigations into Russian collusion with the Trump campaign, unthinkable obstruction of justice, and numerous scandals directed at the president and his inner circle. The Oval Office dynamic shifted from counselors with experienced advice to aides and advisors whose ethically questionable modus operandi and omertà-like loyalty to the president elucidated concern that America's highest office is being run by a crime syndicate.

The monumental, spectacular outcome of this debacle is yet to come. Ultimately, we'll either set our country on a collision course for dissolution or become stronger than ever before. This time, the choice is up to all of us. Will we accept the results of the 2016 election sitting down or will we stand up and fight for the country we want to be? Will we allow the archaic processes that caused us to award one candidate with the popular vote and another with the presidency to divide us or will we demand a change? We have a choice: to learn from history and improve our chances for a better tomorrow or accept our demise by opting not to look back.

Make America Stronger Together Again addresses the presidential campaign of the century, looking in-depth at what happened and what has occurred since. (It is impossible to leave the politics out of the equation and partisan activities will be discussed in actuality, not in the abstract.) This book not only addresses the feelings of angst as Donald Trump ascended into America's highest office, but it discusses the potential for bringing Americans back together again after the most heated and divisive election in modern history. It ties together the lessons of the past with the promise of the future. Ultimately, this book lays out an agenda for

INTRODUCTION

what we can learn from the 2016 election and how we can work together to build an America that is truly Stronger Together.

PART ONE: LOOKING BACK

CHAPTER ONE: HILLARY RODHAM CLINTON

Everyone knows the woman. Her name is synonymous with the White House and the American presidency, though she has never held that highest office. Regardless of where you live in the world, the socio-economic class you exist in, or to what political motivations you ascribe, you know who she is...she's Hillary Rodham Clinton. She's America's First Lady of the 1990's, a champion for women and girls, a fierce advocate for healthcare, a pantsuit aficionado, and a formidable icon of the world's preeminent and most influential superpower. She's a mother, a wife, a grandmother, a lawyer, a politician, and a role model for young people around the globe...yet she is so much more than just that.

Hillary Diane Rodham was born of humble beginnings, unlike the distinguished and infamous caricature the world has come to love. She grew up, not in a shiny gold-gilded estate in New York's finest neighborhood, but in a modest Park Ridge home in the Chicago suburbs. Her parents, devoted benchmarks of middle-class Americana, were driven to raise their children in a world that was better and brighter than their own respective past. It's what made Hillary the woman she is to this day, her roots in the American working-class and her family's direct influence toward raising a future First Lady, U.S. Senator, Secretary of State, and the first female candidate for President of the United States by a major political party.

Dorothy, Hillary's mother, was abandoned as a child and at 14 years of age was forced to work as a housemaid to support herself. She relied on the encouragement of others, receiving kindness and inspiration from those around her – a lesson she passed on to her children. Hillary's father Hugh (a U.S. Navy Chief Petty Officer) instilled drive and ambition in his daughter, teaching her to reach for the stars and never give up on her dreams. Together her parents inspired her to serve others, to live by Methodist teachings including the Wesleyan Rule of Life, and to recognize that everyone needs a champion and a fair chance to succeed.

Growing up in a suburb of a very diverse megalopolis like Chicago gave young Hillary a humble respect for others. People from all backgrounds and all walks of life lived in close proximity to each other and melded a uniquely American culture. Thanks to the youth minister of the Methodist church that her family attended, young Hillary Rodham was inspired to pursue social justice reform. She even met Reverend Dr. Martin Luther King Jr. in 1962. Hillary was raised to accept others for who they are and recognize their individuality. Later in life these core values, instilled in her from a young age, drove her to fight for minorities, families, and children.

After graduating in the top 95 percentile of her high school class, a young and intellectually brilliant Rodham moved to the Boston suburbs for college. In Massachusetts, she attended the all-female Wellesley College, studying political science. While initially a prominent conservative and soon president of the Wellesley College Republicans, Hillary began to change her political leanings in the wake of the Civil Rights Movement and the Vietnam War. By her third year, Rodham was supporting Eugene McCarthy, a Democrat, in the 1968 presidential elections. She took on a more aggressive role in student government, organizing fellow students to pressure Wellesley to support hiring a more diverse staff and to encourage more African American students to attend the prestigious school.

By the time her Bachelor's degree was in sight, Hillary had earned the respect of her peers and was asked by her classmates and the school administration to be the College's first student speaker at the 1969 commencement ceremony. A graduate with honors, she delivered to her fellow students an inspirational oration that criticized Republican Senator Edward Brooks, who incidentally was the "official" commencement speaker. Her passionate speech garnered copious support from the crowd of graduates and earned her 7 minutes of applause at its end. It also brought Hillary national attention and put her in the spotlight, providing a platform for future political success.

After Wellesley, Rodham relocated to Connecticut to attend Yale Law School. While there, she worked on social justice and children's issues, as well as participating in a host of political gigs including the 1972 presidential campaign of George McGovern. After attaining a Juris Doctor and meeting her future husband, William "Bill" Jefferson Clinton, Rodham got to work on youth and family issues, first as an attorney at the Children's Defense Fund and later at the University of Arkansas, Fayetteville.

She dedicated herself to expanding assistance for children and families, going door-to-door advocating for children with disabilities who were denied entry into their local schools. She stood up for young boys in South Carolina, who were thrown in jail cells alongside serious adult criminals. She investigated racism in Alabama schools, going undercover to prove academies were violating federal integration laws by exposing them for illegal segregation practices. She even organized a legal aid clinic, providing services to the impoverished and imprisoned in Arkansas.

In 1978, when Bill successfully won his bid for the Arkansas Gubernatorial race, Hillary became the state's First Lady. Not willing to sit on the sidelines, she was the first First Lady to hold a position outside of the political realm, maintaining her activism for the disenfranchised. In addition to her work at the Rose Law Firm, Hillary also had an official role in the Arkansas government, leading policy on health care for impoverished Arkansans and launching several education initiatives.

The Clintons remained in Little Rock during the 12 years of Bill's Gubernatorial tenure, yet they always had an eye on Washington. Having earlier failed the DC bar exam, Hillary never lost interest in national politics. She worked under the Carter Administration, where she was appointed director of the Legal Services Corporation. Later she actively lobbied the Reagan Administration to prevent funding cuts to that organization.

In 1992, Clinton became the center of national attention once again, this time as her husband entered the 1992 campaign for president. During a tumultuous primary that brought media attention to contested infidelities in the Clinton's marriage, Hillary's prominence grew. She became outspoken on the role of women in politics and refused to take the conventional function of a candidate's wife, choosing instead to go on the campaign trail as both an advisor and a surrogate. During the campaign, she fired up the traditionalists by responding to concerns of her unconventional responsibilities as Arkansas' First Lady arguing, "I suppose I could have stayed home, baked cookies and had teas." It was commonly implied on the campaign that the Clintons were more of a political team than previous candidates for the office, and a vote for Clinton would be a vote for both Bill and Hillary.

While the campaign never officially played the "co-presidents card", it was evident that Hillary would hold an expansive role in a Clinton Administration. Bill even alluded to the wide responsibility Hillary would have as First Lady, suggesting that by voting for him America would get "two for the price of one". Pundits on both sides have argued that this feeling by the electorate may have been the driver for the decisive victory in the Primary and General Elections. Immediately after the '92 election, the conservative attacks began, only becoming more ferocious as the Clinton Administration broke new barriers and created economic growth.

Mrs. Clinton never enjoyed the image as "Bill's Accessory" – the stereotypical role of previous first ladies. Once Bill was elected, Hillary expected the media and the country to accept that she was a different kind of presidential spouse, just as her husband was a new kind of president. She proved that by pressing her husband to select the most diverse cabinet in American history composed of a nearly 50-50 ratio of men to women. She also secured an official position for herself, beyond the White House "hostess and interior decorator roles" often attributed to the American First Lady.

Hillary was tasked with numerous policy issues during her husband's administration. Unlike previous First Ladies who maintained office space in the residence or the East Wing, Hillary was the first First Lady to have an office in the West Wing of the White House, the presidential nerve center. She chaired the Clinton Administration's 1993 task force in building a legislative coalition with the goal of passing universal healthcare for all Americans. After the 1993 healthcare bill was declared dead, she championed the effort to establish the Children's Health Insurance Program (CHIP), an initiative that ultimately covered over 9 million children.

In 1995, the First Lady traveled to China to participate in the United Nations Fourth World Conference on Women in Beijing. She gave a spotlight keynote address, demanding equal rights for women. "If there is one message that echoes forth from this conference, let it be that human rights are women's rights and women's rights are human rights, once and for all", Clinton proclaimed. The speech immediately gave the young First Lady an international following and propelled her onto the global political stage, an important characteristic for a future political role.

The White House years brought the Clintons many challenges and put unspeakable strain on their marriage. An investigation alleged the president and first lady had been involved in a fraudulent real estate development, causing the Justice Department to impanel a grand jury and an independent special counsel to investigate. This Ken Starr investigation into the Whitewater development uncovered a more personal scandal involving inappropriate behavior between President Clinton and a White House intern. While the House of Representatives impeached the president, the Senate failed to convict, thereby acquitting him. Her husband's reputation might have been briefly tarnished, however, Hillary wasn't done with politics. In 2000, she officially entered the race for the U.S. Senate seat in New York.

Hillary's congressional campaign involved a statewide listening tour, a prominent tactic used in later campaigns to engage with the voting public. She listened to the hearts of her would-be constituents and built a rapport with the citizenry of New York. As a result, the state voted 55-43 percent in her favor and she became the only First Lady to serve concurrently in another office and the only former First Lady to serve in an elected office.

Clinton won reelection in 2006 by a larger margin than her 2000 victory. She secured critical funding to rebuild New York City in the aftermath of the September 11th attacks and led the charge for security improvements throughout New York State. She worked across the proverbial aisle, finding common ground with conservative Senators and building important alliances to pass meaningful bipartisan legislation. She took on a new role building a progressive wing on the left to match the conservative forces she had faced during her husband's campaigns and presidency. In doing so, she maintained her prominence and was considered a shoo-in for the 2008 Democratic presidential nomination.

Following her announcement in January of 2007, Hillary was the presumptive Democratic nominee for president in the eyes of many political commentators. She had experience that was unmatched by the field of candidates she was running against. Yet her campaign lacked the passion and vigor of fellow Senator Barack Obama (D-IL), a relative newcomer to national politics. What she had in experience, he had in a message of "change to believe in". While she took the New Hampshire primary in a surprise victory, cleaned up on Super Tuesday in the biggest delegate states, and ultimately won the popular vote, she lost the delegate lead to Senator Obama.

Obama was successful in 2008 because he inspired hope and offered a new change that would pivot from an America that had slumped into a financial recession. Clinton didn't have a way to differentiate herself from the Obama "fired up, ready to go" drive and make her campaign as inspiring as the Democratic powerhouse that handed Senator Obama the presidency. Clinton's chief distinction was her experience and her gender. However, unlike the passion to elect the first African American president, many Americans believed the country would elect a woman as president in their lifetime. The opportunity to elect an African American to the Oval Office seemed considerably less likely in the future. Ultimately, that attitude launched Obama into the history books and left Clinton without a path to victory – her presidential ambitions would have to wait. Gender took a backseat to race in 2008 and eventually charged the future candidacy of Clinton in 2016.

On June 7th, 2008 in the National Building Museum in Washington D.C. and with her husband, mother, and daughter at her side, Hillary suspended her campaign. She conceded victory to Barack Obama, formally endorsing the Illinois Senator. Although she was considered a favorable running mate for Obama in the General Election, she instead became a fierce surrogate alongside her husband President Clinton. Both advocated for the Obama-Biden ticket nationwide, with Hillary even nominating Senator Obama on the floor of the DNC Convention in Denver. There she fervently requested the delegates nominate him by acclamation during the roll call of the states.

In the weeks after Senator Obama's significant win over Republican Senator John McCain, Clinton was offered the role of Secretary of State in the new administration. Although she initially refused the offer, ostensibly several times including to the president-elect himself, she ultimately accepted the call to lead the diplomatic efforts to restore America's image abroad. Once again, Hillary became the only First Lady to serve in a president's cabinet and also became the third woman to hold the esteemed title of U.S. Secretary of State.

At the State Department, Secretary Clinton led efforts to reset the American foreign policy agenda and bring to a close the divisions of international relations caused by the U.S. invasion of Iraq in 2003. Clinton traveled nearly a million miles around the globe rebuilding broken international relationships, forging new partnerships, and brokering new business agreements for U.S. corporations. She developed new initiatives that focused on supporting international aid programs and empowering young women and girls, especially in areas of continued regional conflict. Clinton demanded international recognition of LGBTQ rights, borrowing from her Beijing remarks in proclaiming, "gay rights are human rights". She advised the president on important foreign policy affairs and led the effort to convince President Obama to proceed with the raid on Al Qaeda terror cell leader Osama Bin Laden's Abbottabad compound. Clinton also formed an international coalition to impose economic sanctions on Iran, laying the framework for the Iran Nuclear Deal, which was agreed to under her successor, Secretary John Kerry.

Clinton's tenure at Foggy Bottom is most notable for her use of Smart Power diplomacy, a combination of the conventional soft and hard power approaches to international relations. In utilizing diplomacy (Soft Power) backed up with the threat of military action (Hard Power) the Clinton Smart Power diplomacy model was hyper-effective in restoring America's image around the globe and building peaceful coalitions to tackle human rights violations, poverty, regional conflict, and inadequate healthcare.

The public has always seen Hillary Clinton in the spotlight, keeping an eye on the highest office in America. Perceptions, although split nearly evenly between staunch supporters and avid critics, have always been high as her record, tenacity, and experience in public service support her ambitions for political office. Few see her as a person and not just another political candidate. Although she has been named the world's most admired woman a record 22 times (16 times consecutively), polls give her a favorability in the low 40s to high 30s. President Obama has called her "joyful", citing her "infectious laugh" as an added bonus to her sharp understanding of complicated challenges. Others view her as fiercely competitive, Machiavellian, even scripted. Those who have been touched by her, through her advocacy and service, maintain that she is comforting, gracious, thoughtful and kind. In their eyes, Clinton embodies the "country of we, not country of me" principle she was taught as a child.

After four years as head of the diplomatic arm of American government, Clinton resigned the office to work on other projects, including her husband's foundation. At the Clinton Foundation, she spearheaded several initiatives, focusing mainly on her passion for women and girls empowerment, and began organizing her thoughts from her time in public office into a book and a potential presidential campaign. Even before the June 2014 release of her memoir, *Hard Choices*, Clinton was being polled as the likely frontrunner for the 2016 presidential election. Questions at book signings often asked which title she preferred, Mrs. President or Madam President. In fact, since Obama's win in 2008, pundits on the left and right made predictions that she would be his successor as the Democratic candidate in eight years.

On April 12th, 2015, Hillary Clinton made her official announcement in a two and a half minute video declaring:

"I'm running for president! Americans have fought their way back from tough economic times. But the deck is still stacked in favor of those at the top. Everyday Americans need a champion, and I want to be that champion. So you can do more than just get by. You can get ahead, and stay ahead. Because when families are strong, America is strong. So I'm hitting the road to earn your vote, because it's your time. And I hope you'll join me on this journey."

-Excerpts from Clinton's Announcement Video (April 12, 2015)

CHAPTER TWO: DONALD J. TRUMP

He's known as "The Donald", "Trump", and "the Boss". He's a property developer, turned reality star, turned politician. He's been in the spotlight for decades and has been a potential candidate for president time and time again. While his hypothetical candidacy was always just the butt of a bad joke, it quickly became real during the most intense and discordant election of modern times.

Donald John Trump was born to Fred and Mary Anne Trump on June 14, 1946, in New York's Queens Borough. His father, a prominent member of the New York elite, was a developer of real estate properties in the greater New York City metropolitan area. Originally focused on military barracks and government-contracted buildings, Fred Trump quickly dove into the lucrative business of building middle-class housing targeted at veterans returning home from the European theater of World War II. By the 1950s he had transitioned to building apartment complexes, row houses, and low income "projects" for families living on government subsidies.

Donald Trump grew up in the family business, leaving home in his early teens for the New York Military Academy. Away from distractions, Trump's five years there gave him a focused boarding school education and, according to Trump, an insight into the military beyond what he could have obtained by actually serving in the armed forces. He once boasted that he received "more training militarily than a lot of the guys that go into the military". Due to the strictness of the school's administration, Trump did well at NYMA and became a captain in charge of a top tier company of cadets.

Upon graduating from boarding school, Trump began taking college classes at the Jesuit-Catholic Fordham University in New York City. Trump transferred to the University of Pennsylvania in 1966, where he took classes in business, including a few courses through the Wharton School at U-Penn. While attending college, the collegiate spent little time outside of class on the school campus. Instead, he was involved in his father's real estate business, "Elizabeth Trump and Son". During his years at Fordham and the University of Pennsylvania, Donald obtained student deferments from the Selective Service System and a 1-Y deferment for bone spurs by providing medical records to the local draft board. Those deferrals prevented the trust-fund-supported and very affluent Trump from being conscripted into service during the Vietnam War.

Trump's business career took off after graduation with the help of his father who supplied his son with a personal loan of one million dollars. According to Trump, he was given the money to invest in real estate ventures in New York City. Recognizing the scope of his father's influence in the Queens and Brooklyn boroughs, Donald chose to focus on Manhattan where he wouldn't compete with his father or lie in his shadow.

Donald demonstrated a natural knack for business and quickly made a name for himself in the Manhattan development world. While investors were shy to support projects in the struggling borough, Trump found loopholes and "get-a-rounds" to secure funding. On one early project (the Commodore Hotel), Trump was unable to secure the necessary financing and tax incentives from the city. Due to his lack of experience, banks and financial institutions similarly didn't trust him with an expensive investment like the Commodore. So Trump lined up Hyatt Hotels to run the new venture and successfully secured backing for the project.

Throughout his business career, Donald (master of the business deal) often found ways to get around hurdles that slowed down a project or that would reduce his financial risk. In an early joint venture with Harrah's (then owned by Holiday Inns Inc.), Trump promised to build a parking ramp for a casino in exchange for financing. Few financial institutions were willing to gamble on Trump or the emerging Atlantic City gaming scene. Trump Plaza was a deal where Trump would develop and co-own the casino/hotel with Holiday Inns while Harrah's would operate the property. On opening day, no parking garage had been constructed and Trump, changing his mind, continuously delayed erecting the proposed ramp as long as Harrah's operated the casino. Without parking, the property floundered, causing Harrah's-Holiday Inns to sell their share of the investment to Trump who immediately built the parking ramp once the deal closed. With the attached parking garage, Trump Plaza became a successful project.

Like the Hyatt-Commodore Hotel project, Trump – the master dealer – was always looking out for his best interests. Critics suggested that from the beginning he hoped to work with Harrah's to secure the financing, furtively planning to buy them out all along. Commentators even claim that Trump never intended fulfilling his obligation of erecting the parking ramp until Harrah's was out of the deal. These acts of "real estate theater", as Trump's approach has been called, didn't generally serve well for his business associates. Donald didn't work well in partnerships, focusing on his personal priorities rather than a larger vision shared with a team. Numerous deals were made, some even terminated, because Trump used unconventional approaches to meet his goals at the embarrassment or loss of his partners.

Money, the Trump brand, his business empire, and the Trump family are perhaps the most important assets in Donald's life. Trump has five children with three wives. With Ivana Zelníčková, Trump's first wife, Donald fathered three children: Donald Jr., Ivanka, and Eric. Trump hailed the birth of daughter Tiffany during his marriage to actress Marla Maples. In 2005, Trump married fashion model Melania Knauss, and soon after the couple welcomed Barron into the family. Trump's eldest three children all play important roles in the family real estate conglomerate, The Trump Organization. Tiffany, raised by her mother Marla Maples, attended college away from the Trump family's New York City headquarters and has largely been left outside of the business inner circle. Barron, the youngest of the five, lives at home with Donald and Melania, often spending time with his father in the office downstairs. In addition to Trump's wives, children, and father, Donald's other family members have had a profound impact on his public and personal life. Brother Fred Trump Jr., who tragically died from alcoholism, influenced Donald to become a teetotaler – abstaining from the alcohol, tobacco, and drugs commonly abused by wealthy playboys.

The Trump brand is perhaps the most valued possession in the New York made real estate tycoon's portfolio. When his personal finances dried up and his ventures started to collapse, Trump began franchising his name. While many properties around the globe feature the Trump brand prominently on their masthead and marquee, Donald has only minimal or no equity in the building or the property under it. Instead, hotels, skyscrapers, and other businesses license the name "TRUMP", paying the Trump Organization to use the name's lucrative brand. In return, the Trump Organization promotes the properties with Donald acting as a mascot and figurehead of the assets.

This franchise approach came after years of struggle for Trump's businesses that included multiple bankruptcies. Numerous casinos of incredible size competing with each other in focused regions, a failing New York to DC air shuttle service, and a host of other ventures stretched Donald Trump's financial strength to its breaking point. Although he never filed for personal bankruptcy, six of his businesses were forced to undergo Chapter 11 bankruptcy protection and ultimately corporate reorganization. Though the individual ventures floundered, Trump maintained personal liquidity and often benefitted from the insolvencies by playing with bankruptcy statutes and finding loopholes to write off the failed projects. Recognizing the value of his celebrity, he quickly turned his brand into the backbone of his business. Today Trump's name, synonymous with glamor, glitz, and wealth, is one of his biggest moneymakers.

Donald Trump's empire of business ventures is huge and very

diversified. His name is on everything, from Trump Ice bottled water to Donald J. Trump Signature Collection menswear, even a model management company and the SUCCESS fragrance line. Nevertheless, his core business remains in real estate investments including numerous properties owned or managed by the Trump Organization, partnerships with other developers, and golf courses in the United States, the United Kingdom, and the United Arab Emirates.

Donald is proud of his family business and keeps close watch over messaging and press. He has even been known to use aliases from time to time to personally share information with media outlets and build hype for his current projects. When he was selling spaces in his namesake Trump Tower property, "John Barron" (one of Trump's aliases) suggested to the news that Princess Diana was looking at securing an apartment in the building. This pseudonym was also used in press junkets for several other business dealings including the potential purchase of the Cleveland Indians in the 1980s.

A decade after the John Barron years, Trump introduced a new pseudonym, "John Miller". Miller, supposedly a publicist of The Donald, returned calls to media outlets that sought interviews with the well-off entrepreneur. Although never fully admitted by Trump, each of the alter egos clearly was Donald attempting to answer questions incognito. Barron and Miller both had similar voices, which matched Trump in tone and tenor. Neither was ever seen in person, only answering questions over the phone. In a lawsuit in 1990, Trump did say he believed on occasion that he used the name John Barron. Interesting to note, Trump's youngest son is also named Barron. Television anchors generally accepted the nom de guerre speaking with them over the phone as an extension of Donald's unconventional character, overprotective of the Trump name.

While Donald Trump's professional brand has always been tied to his personality, he built his star power in his partnership with NBC as the host, producer, and star of *The Apprentice* reality TV program. The boardroom blockbuster show pitted contestants vying for a role in one of Trump's business ventures. The production inaugurated Trump's famous catchphrase "You're fired!" – an exclamation that Donald would make to culminate an episode and send a contestant home. *The Apprentice* grew a huge following and eventually led to spinoffs including a Martha Stewart hosted *Apprentice* in 2005 and *The Celebrity Apprentice* in 2008.

Trump's career in the spotlight as the host of *The Apprentice* was just the beginning though. Asked often if he would consider running for president, Trump consistently turned down the suggestions. Although never fully ruling out a run in the future, he enjoyed the constant hype, frequently teasing the press with the idea of a Trump presidency. According to the business tycoon, he tossed around the idea of competing on a third party ticket several times, ultimately choosing to direct his attention to his business dealings instead. Donald donated to candidates on both sides of the political aisle, including to then-U.S. Senator Hillary Clinton. He also made appearances at many of Washington DC's most auspicious occasions. Trump was never silent about his positions on political issues or politicians, sharing his thoughts with the media and on his NBC reality show.

As far back as March of 2011, Donald Trump stirred up a political thorn suggesting that President Barack Obama was hiding something on his birth certificate and alluding to the president's choice not to publicly release the document. After claims by pundits and politicians alike supporting Trump's belief that President Obama wasn't born in Hawaii, Trump joined the "Birther Movement" in calling for the release of documentation that proved the President's citizenship. Obama released his long-form birth certificate on April 27th, 2011 putting the scandal to rest, much to the chagrin of the Birthers. Trump nevertheless continued the narrative into the 2012 election cycle by offering to donate $5 million dollars (later increased to $50 million) to charity if Obama released his passport and college applications to the public. That offer apparently expired before Trump was obligated to cut a check, with the businessman still appearing to believe there was dishonesty surrounding Obama's U.S. citizenship claims.

President Obama and late night comedians poked fun at Trump's continued belief that the 44th President was born outside the United States. The president especially enjoyed joking about the unsubstantiated claims – alleging he was born in Kenya, was a Muslim, and that the opening scene to Disney's *The Lion King* was his birth video. Trump took credit for the Obama Administration's release of the long-form birth certificate (the short-form certificate was released by the Obama campaign in 2008) and used the perpetuated conspiracy to increase his popularity with those on the right. Due to his status boost from the birther conspiracy, Trump considered a 2012 campaign in the Republican primaries, choosing eventually not to run. He nevertheless spent millions between 2012 and 2013 researching a possible candidacy in the future.

In 2015, after making headlines by refusing to commit to another season of *The Apprentice*, Trump called a press conference at Trump Tower two days after his June 16th birthday. Considered a tawdry entrance, Donald and his wife Melania descended the escalator in the Trump Tower lobby to officially announce his candidacy for the Republican nomination for president. He laid out his campaign platform in his announcement speech, calling attention to global terrorism and suggesting a goal of bringing jobs back to the United States. He pointed to his business "chops" as experience in leadership that would be unmatched by rival Republicans and Democrats, and he promoted his personal wealth as a signal of his success in the business world.

Trump's speech immediately took criticism, not only for his harsh language but also his degrading remarks about immigration when he declared:

"When Mexico sends its people, they're not sending their best. They're not sending you...They're sending people that have lots of problems, and they're bringing those problems with us. They're bringing drugs. They're bringing crime. They're rapists. And some, I assume, are good people."

–Excerpts from **Trump's Announcement at Trump Tower** (June 16, 2015)

With that Donald Trump launched his campaign for the presidency with the aspiration to "Make America Great Again" (MAGA).

CHAPTER THREE: DEMOCRATIC PRIMARY – THE RACE FOR IOWA, THE "DAMN EMAILS", AND HISTORY MADE!

Each of the Democratic contenders began their campaigns in the late spring and early summer of 2015, entering the political season later than the Republicans vying for the GOP nomination. All eyes were watching after the announcement of Hillary Clinton as to who would be next entering the race. Within days, U.S. Senator Bernard Sanders (I-VT) and Maryland Governor Martin O'Malley joined the Democratic campaign crusade. As the three first candidates circled the early states, they were constantly barraged with questions from the press about potential opponents yet to enter. Rumors swirled that Al Gore, Michelle Obama, or even George Clooney were considering a run, perhaps due to the comparison of the wide span of candidates who competed in the 2008 Democratic primary season. Also on the shortlist were Vice President Joe Biden and U.S. Senator Elizabeth Warren (D-

MA). By mid-summer, Rhode Island Governor Lincoln Chafee and U.S. Senator Jim Webb (D-VA) joined the three major candidates.

Fresh out of the gate, Hillary Clinton faced a scandal with the potential to derail her Oval Office aspirations before she even made her first appearance as a presidential candidate. For months, Republicans on Capitol Hill and across conservative media derided the Secretary's use of personal email during her tenure as the nation's chief diplomat. They argued that Clinton's choice to host her email on a secure server in her home's basement put American secrets at risk. As the chief architect of U.S. foreign policy, Clinton would have had access to extensive government confidences, many so highly classified they were couriered to her office in lockboxes handcuffed to the wrist of the government messenger delivering them. Although the partisan smoke screen suggested the potential for a national security incident, Hillary's personal server was never compromised.

Nothing was immoral or illegal about a pool table added to the billiard hall of 1900s River City Iowa. Yet in Meredith Willson's The Music Man, Professor Harold Hill riled up the town when he implied a pool table was sinful just because it was different than what people were used to. Clinton's use of a private email server was no more illegal or malicious than a pool table in a billiard hall. Nevertheless, Republicans blew the email debate out of proportion, making a mountain out of a "molehill" by suggesting that because it was not a common practice, it was criminal. Senior campaign advisors always knew there would be a hurdle Clinton would have to overcome. Ever since the 1992 Presidential Campaign that elected her husband, the general public had an uncomfortable feeling about Hillary. Her campaign even had a nickname for the undeserved feelings of uncertainty toward the former First Lady, "TSAHIJDL" or "There's Something About Her I Just Don't Like". Regardless of her dedication to the country, a scandal of some kind would have to surface, keeping the feelings of hesitation and indecision in check for the Clinton critics...this time it was her handling of emails.

In the eyes of the Clinton campaign, right-wing media and Republican politicians were making something out of nothing. Even after similar uses of private email by George W. Bush Administration officials (including Secretary of State Colin Powell) surfaced in the media, Republicans stayed focused on Clinton alone. Perhaps her female gender suggested she would be weaker at keeping secrets than her male predecessor...or perhaps it was just because she was the Democratic frontrunner and Republicans were scared that without a damaging scandal, Clinton would easily win in the November 2016 election. Regardless, the emails would continually stir up doubt about the Democratic candidate that later had the explosive potential to change history.

As is usual in a presidential campaign, the candidates (all five) made appearances in the early states (Iowa, New Hampshire, Nevada, South Carolina) and went to liberal hotspots to raise campaign capital. Summer progressed to fall and a few of the possible candidates, in particular Joe Biden and Elizabeth Warren, had not publicly stated their intentions. Calls by liberals for Biden to enter the race increased going into the first Democratic debate. Before the debate, the pleas were "Go Joe Go"; after the debate, they became "No Joe No!" With news that the Vice President might make an imminent announcement on October 20th, America asked "So Joe...Go?" The following day, October 21st, Biden publicly announced that he would not seek the presidency and the resulting chant was "No, Joe No Go." Senator Warren also declined to enter consideration, though neither she nor Biden were quick to endorse a declared candidate.

All five of the progressive hopefuls attended the first Democratic Debate in Las Vegas in October of 2015. AC360's Anderson Cooper moderated the event hosted by CNN and Facebook. The debate gave the candidates their first attempt to appeal to the American people directly and outline their platforms. It also helped show the range of differences between the candidates and gave the viewer a glimpse of how each handled tough questions on their feet. Opposite the off-the-wall banter on the Republican stage a week prior, the frontrunner Hillary Clinton came out strong. She demonstrated her domestic and foreign policy credentials along with an ability to counterpunch attacks from her opponents. Bernie Sanders, the surprise threat, proved himself as the candidate to take on the political establishment. O'Malley, a well-spoken, energetic, and effective leader, demonstrated his merits and made it clear he was deserving of a podium alongside Clinton and Sanders. On the sidelines, Chafee and Webb underperformed, extinguishing the brief glimmer of a chance for either of the two respected politicians to clinch the nomination.

Two weeks after the first debate, the race had narrowed – three experienced leaders – three energetic campaigns. Bernie's message of financial inequality resonated with young voters, especially recent college and high school graduates. Clinton's knack for clear answers to tough questions gave her continued momentum, pulling in endorsements from major political icons in the Democratic Party and important media organizations in the early states. Martin O'Malley held on, struggling to find his place between Sanders' progressive movement and Hillary's more centrist base.

His efforts gained supporters who sought something between the two headliners.

Overall, the Democratic Debates had interesting high moments that only mildly competed with the wild fiascos transpiring at the televised Republican debates. During the CNN/Facebook matchup, Bernie answered a question regarding Clinton's use of a private email server as Secretary of State forcefully articulating, "Let me say something that may not be great politics, but I think the Secretary is right…the American people are sick and tired of hearing about your damn emails!" On two separate occasions, Clinton returned late to the debate stage after a commercial break, noting that it took her longer than her male counterparts. The second time she returned tardy, Hillary was met with thunderous applause even though co-moderator David Muir (ABC News) had already started asking the next set of questions. Later in the evening, Muir asked Clinton about her support by American businesses and Wall Street, questioning whether Corporate America should "love Hillary." Clinton responded arguing, "Everybody should love her!" Later adding a popular culture reference in her closing argument, she exclaimed, "Thank you, goodnight, and may the force be with you."

A shooting in Oregon on October 1st, 2015, drove the conversation on the road and on the debate stage to gun control. Clinton and O'Malley both attacked Senator Sanders' record on guns, noting his opposition of the landmark Brady Bill of 1993. They also questioned the Senator's stance, allowing Amtrak passengers to pack guns in their checked luggage onboard the railroad's network of train routes. Clinton implied the Senator's acquiescence towards the accessibility of guns on trains indicated support for the NRA's agenda. Meanwhile, Governor O'Malley fought valiantly to assert his background as the Mayor of Baltimore and Chief Executive of Maryland. In both capacities, he instituted numerous gun control laws and decreased crime during his tenure. Unfortunately, O'Malley's narrative was diminished by the death of Freddie Gray, who died in Baltimore Police Department's custody earlier in the year. Clinton passionately called for more gun reforms, arguing it was "time for the country to stand up against the NRA".

In addition to guns, race relations and illegal drug use resonated as major undertones of the Democratic primary season. Divisive rhetoric from the Republicans running for office made headlines, connecting crimes on the street with excessive rates of incarceration of African Americans within urban metropolises. The advocacy group, Black Lives Matter, made repeated appearances at campaign rallies and events, demanding the Democratic candidates publicly assert "Black Lives Matter!" The growing American opioid crisis only intensified the discourse requiring all three campaigns to double down on support for drug awareness and mental health programs.

While the Democrats were facing off against each other with the hopes of leading the opposition against a Republican challenger, Wall Street quickly became their enemy on debate stages and across the campaign trail. Bernie railed against the Obama Administration's bank bailout in the wake of the 2008 recession, demanding that America's next president "break up the big banks". O'Malley and Sanders called out Hillary's paid speeches to Goldman Sachs and other Wall Street powerhouses, suggesting she was in the pocket of the big banks. Clinton countered, arguing she had been tough as a Senator on Wall Street and that banks had invited her to speak about her experiences as Secretary of State, not as a quid pro quo for their future protection from legislative reform. On the stump, Bernie's antipathy of the banks became a stronger message, forcing Clinton to rally against the banks.

Trying to get a word in edgewise, O'Malley called for the reinstatement of Glass-Steagall, four provisions in the U.S. Banking Act of 1933 that prevented commercial banks from engaging in securities exchange. (The landmark legislation also created the Federal Deposit Insurance Corporation which guaranteed bank deposits up to $250,000, essentially preventing runs on banks and severing the link between investment and commercial banking so as to prevent an economic recession or depression.) In light of the partial repeal of the legislation in 1999 likely contributing to the 2008 financial crisis, O'Malley challenged Clinton and Sanders to make such policy a part of their platforms too. Clinton called for a wider policy than just reforming the big banks, adding investment firms, insurance companies, and hedge funds to her proposal.

All three candidates in the prelude to the start of the primaries argued that they had much in common and their platforms differed greatly from the Republicans running. Nonetheless, there were clear disagreements. Bernie called for far-left ideas, including free college and universal healthcare, while Clinton and O'Malley defended continuing the initiatives of the Obama Administration and expanding them to meet their objectives. Sanders' out of the mainstream thinking forced Clinton to move left and constantly defend her flank – the Obama coalition that would be the Democratic backbone in the fall.

While all three liberals broadly agreed on foreign policy, Sanders and O'Malley consistently attacked Clinton for her support of the Iraq War as a Senator in 2003. They questioned her tendency to support regime change and chided her continued reiteration of supporting Obama's agenda while maintaining a different opinion privately. Clinton made great strides in foreign policy debates though, relying on her years of experience to outperform her opponents. She used real victories as validating representations of her ability to execute on the world stage, including her support of Obama's decision to take out Al Qaeda terror leader Osama Bin Laden in 2011.

In 2016, the Democratic Party employed an indirect system of electing a presidential nominee. Primaries and caucuses in every state and territory utilized a proportional representation system. Votes were allocated by the ratio of the states' registered Democrats that each candidate had won in the primary. So if a candidate received 50% of the vote in a state, they'd earn 50% of the state's pledged delegates. (The Iowa Caucus was an exception, proportionately awarding fifteen statewide delegates and the remaining twenty-nine to the winner of each of Iowa's four Congressional districts. Each district was apportioned a set number of delegates – D_1 had 8, D_2 had 8, D_3 had 7, and D_4 had 6. Since District Three (7) and the statewide (15) delegate counts were odd numbers, the winner in a close (51-49) result would receive one extra delegate. Most states bound (required) their delegates to vote at the Democratic National Convention (the DNC being the official nominating conference of the Democratic Party) for the candidate who won the district they represented. Bound delegates could only change their support to a different candidate after the first round of voting, should no candidate receive a majority (50% +1) of the party's total delegates at the DNC convention. States also had unpledged superdelegates, delegates not bound to vote for the candidate their state supported. Of the total available delegates,

15% or 714 were unpledged super-delegates, comprised of Democratic Congressmen, Senators, Governors, DNC leaders, and state party leadership. Most unpledged superdelegates granted their vote to a candidate they personally endorsed, some waiting to give their vote to the winner of their state's primary contest.

In the 2016 election, a candidate needed to acquire a combination of bound and non-binding delegates, totaling 2,382 to become the nominee. Pledged delegates were proportionate to the number of Electoral College electors given to each state under the U.S. Census. However, according to the complicated Democratic Primary rules, the date of each primary contest and the proportion of Democratic voters in each state, based on the three prior elections, determined the final delegate allocation each state received.

The Hillary For America campaign was the heavy favorite in the summer of 2015, but by the time the first primary rolled around in early 2016, the race had narrowed. All of the candidates focused on Iowa and New Hampshire, recognizing that early wins in either state would provide much-needed momentum and financial support going into Super Tuesday and a potentially drawn-out primary season. Unlike the previous presidential election in 2012, the 2016 primary season didn't start until February with the Iowa Caucuses and New Hampshire Primaries.

Iowa is always cold in January and February, but on presidential election years, days seem a little warmer. With excitement in the air and a massive campaign effort underway by each candidate's contingent of volunteers and staff, there was no time to think about cold. Phone banks dialing, canvass teams knocking doors, and signs going up on street after street only intensified the race for the most coveted win of the primary season. In the Bernie, Hillary, and Martin O'Malley campaign offices, samovars of coffee and case stands of energy drinks were refilled constantly. Staffers and volunteers put away as much of the energy-delivering liquids as their bodies would allow, trying to eke out an additional vote anywhere they could before the Iowa Caucuses commenced.

The frontrunners, Hillary and Bernie, each spent millions of dollars flooding the nine media markets that covered the state with advertisements, urging voters to "Feel the Bern" or to be "With Her". All three Democratic hopefuls held rallies and visited thousands of Iowans in every corner of the Hawkeye State. The Clinton campaign officially started with a road trip to Iowa and spent hours hosting listening sessions, town halls, and intimate speaking engagements. Bernie's campaign focused on large rallies with thousands of supporters in attendance. O'Malley's efforts to stay alive in the polls, paired with limited fundraising, required a more hands-on approach. Dwindling campaign coffers forced the Governor to meet with voters on the streets of Des Moines, Cedar Rapids, Davenport, Council Bluffs, Urbandale, Iowa City, and Ames, rather than running expensive T.V. commercials, flooding social media with ads, or holding rallies.

On February 1st, 2016, the moment the campaigns had been waiting for and equally dreading came – the Iowa Caucuses, the early predictor of the 2016 electoral cycle. Hillary Clinton had bested her opponents, leading Bernie Sanders in seven of eight public opinion polls in the days leading up to the election. Tracking and internal polling suggested the race would be close, both top-tier candidates polling within the margin of error of each other. Even entrance polls taken as voters entered polling places before the Caucus showed a tight competition between the two frontrunners with O'Malley trailing significantly. After the photo finish, Clinton narrowly beat Bernie in winning the most state convention delegates, a victory that allocated Secretary Clinton 23 of the state's 44 unpledged delegates to the DNC Convention. Coming in only a quarter percent behind Clinton, Bernie took home the remaining 21 unpledged delegates. (As votes in the Iowa Caucus actually represent votes for the state convention, Clinton received two more delegates than Sanders as her state delegation equivalent margin was 701 to Bernie's 697.) Clinton also received 6 of Iowa's 7 unpledged superdelegates, though most had endorsed her long before the February Caucuses.

The primary bellwether, as usual, played a huge role in shaping the 2016 Democratic nomination contest. O'Malley, who received only 0.54% support in the Caucuses, suspended his campaign narrowing the race to Secretary Clinton and Senator Sanders. Bernie's support among millennial voters gave him an early second place, a position he maintained throughout the primaries. The outcome also gave Hillary the title of first woman to win the Iowa Caucus, although the results were historically close in the final margin of victory. It's very possible that Clinton's margin of victory would have been significantly greater if Iowa utilized a primary (ballot) voting system instead of a caucus (meeting of voters), which historically are biased in favor of younger voters. (Caucuses can last hours and are generally attended by only the staunchest supporters – normally heavily populated by college-aged voters who don't have to arrange childcare to attend.)

The Iowa contest proved what pollsters and pundits had proposed on news media for weeks. Hillary won overwhelmingly in the urban Des Moines metropolitan area (Des Moines, West Des Moines, Urbandale, and Clive) and Bernie won rural counties, in the Quad Cities, and Southeastern Iowa (Davenport and Cedar Rapids). The trend of Clinton wins in urban areas and Sanders' wins in rural communities continued through the primary season with few exceptions.

With O'Malley out of the race, momentum by both the Sanders and Clinton campaigns picked up, especially with the imminent races in New Hampshire, Nevada, and South Carolina just weeks apart. Both campaigns crossed the country fundraising and holding rallies, town halls, and listening sessions. Racing between the Northeast, the West, and Southeast proved tiring and added to the growing tension between the candidates. After a Sanders win in New Hampshire and Clinton wins in Nevada and South Carolina, the professional and conciliatory relationship between the two star power politicians became more indecorous.

Clinton's vast experience in presidential politics gave her an upper hand in the numerous debates of the primary cycle, along with a prepared team designed from the beginning to take on a General Election opponent like Jeb Bush or Ted Cruz. Yet Hillary lacked the energy and sense of social change charisma that Bernie brought to the race. Clinton was not as effective convincing millennials to support her argument that she was the most experienced and best prepared to take on the shrinking Republican field. Bernie's campaign was organized by a younger, less experienced team and was driven by a smaller list of issues, rather than the broad plan for America the Clinton campaign had been promoting. Nevertheless, Bernie's quixotic stance on the core issues of college affordability, campaign finance reform, universal healthcare for all, and Wall Street reorganization gave him a massive following and an energetic college student base. He still trailed Clinton however, as his campaign was limited to only the aforementioned issues. It became clear during the contentious Democratic Primary Debates that Vermont's Jr. Senator was unfamiliar with the intricacies of foreign policy or the hurdles facing his idealistic social agenda.

As the campaign advanced, tensions ran high between both teams and their respective candidates. Ever since a December 2015 breach of a Democratic National Committee server where the Bernie Sanders campaign briefly obtained access to Clinton database records, followed by the DNC cutting off the Sanders campaign's access to their own info, questions of party bias amplified. Sanders' surrogates suggested that the Clinton camp had received help before debates, was getting preferred treatment by party leaders, and that the contest was rigged against Bernie. While Clinton did benefit from wide support of Democratic Party leaders and elected officials, no evidence was ever supplied to expand on the claims of a public bias by the DNC.

The Democratic National Committee clearly wanted to see a Clinton nominee over a Sanders nomination, but outside of a few leaked emails, little was done to internally tip the scale. Several in-house email exchanges between Democratic Party staff does suggest they supported seeing Hillary victorious at the end of the primary process, but no definitive proof of rigging was found. Party insiders and DNC staff, along with Democrats in elected office, widely supported Clinton before the first debate and maintained their support throughout the primary season. Clinton had been a major figure within the party for decades and had earned endorsements after countless appearances over the years at Democratic candidate events. On the other hand, Bernie was a party outsider, choosing to switch from his Independent registration in Congress where he caucused with Democrats and occasionally gave them a majority, to run as a Democrat in order to secure the nomination. Historically, no Independent/non-affiliated candidate has ever come close to securing a majority in the Electoral College vote, making it imperative for a potential candidate to run on a major party (Democratic or Republican) ticket in order to win the race to the White House.

In addition to previous support of Democratic politicians, Clinton also had been a prominent figure in the party since her husband came onto the national stage before his 1992 run for the White House. She had been a fundraiser for the Democratic movement ever since, bringing in funds for female candidates and from women across the country who answered her appeals for contributions. In 2015, the Clinton campaign organized a joint fundraising committee with the DNC to raise money for other Democrats. The Hillary Victory Fund was designed to increase financial contributions feeding congressional elections and the state and local races that would give a Clinton Administration a commanding Democratic majority in Congress and a strong mandate to pass her bold policy initiatives. The Sanders campaign, focused on small contributions (frequently shared to be averaging at $27), couldn't afford to divide cash with a larger, party-led, fundraising arm. Additionally, Sanders had advocated against the DNC's campaign finance tactics and had not been a card-carrying Democrat until the spring of 2015, the moment he announced his intention to run for the Democratic nomination.

As the primaries progressed through the country, Clinton took major victories in 8 of the 12 contests on Super Tuesday. She took a commanding pledged delegate lead from disproportionate victories in Southern states and an insurmountable "super-delegate" total. The Sanders campaign outraised and outspent the Clinton campaign, totaling $219,695,969 to Clinton's $174,101,369 during the primaries. (Instead of spending all her funds against Bernie,

Hillary's campaign was building a war chest for the November General Election.) However, Clinton also had numerous Super-PACs, political action committees, and joint fundraising organizations that supported her. They included the Hillary Victory Fund, Priorities USA, Human Rights Campaign, and Planned Parenthood PAC.

On June 6th, NBC News and the Associated Press called the Democratic Primaries for Hillary Clinton when her pledged and superdelegate total surpassed the 2,382-threshold plurality to become the party's presumptive nominee. Clinton won the popular and delegate vote after a substantial win in the California primaries on June 7th, the eighth anniversary of her 2008 concession speech in the primary against Barack Obama. At her Election Night watch party, Clinton declared victory; her colossal delegate total unsurpassable. Even though she didn't command enough pledged delegates to formally secure the nomination without including superdelegates, the impressive triumph marked a celebrated moment in American history. She finally broke the barrier, which previously had prevented women from leading a major political party in our country. Across the nation, women rejoiced in the mammoth step forward towards ultimately shattering the "highest, hardest glass ceiling" and bringing about gender equity in America's highest political echelon.

Throughout the contentious campaign, Bernie supporters had failed to recognize that Obama's victory wasn't the symbol of the Democratic Party's move to the political left, rather a once-in-a-century electoral miracle. The base of the party wasn't ready yet for Bernie's extremely progressive agenda and wanted a seasoned leader to guarantee a Democrat succeeded President Obama. While party leaders and elected officials supported left-wing ideas like healthcare for all (a common talking point of the Sanders campaign), none believed it would be possible in the immediate four years following the election. Democrats had maintained that Obamacare (Patient Protection and Affordable Care Act) was a step in the right direction and a good starting point in a long fight ahead for universal healthcare. Congressional Democrats who fought alongside then First Lady Clinton knew the idealistic approach to healthcare was harder to achieve than Bernie made it out to be...most still had the scars from trying to pass Clinton's landmark healthcare deal in the 1990s.

Even so, Bernie's campaign had influenced the electorate, demanding that the party platform adopt progressive policies that had been the backbone of his success in college towns and rural America. While his campaign brought millions of young liberals into the political discussion, there is no doubt that Bernie Sanders' campaign damaged Hillary going into the General Election. He forced her further to the political left instead of allowing for a pivot to the center, which would have garnered more support from undecided voters and centrist Republicans.

After defeating Sanders in the primary, Clinton quickly pivoted towards the General Election. She named Virginia junior Senator Tim Kaine as her running mate. Kaine's record, having never lost an election, made him an obvious choice. The U.S. Senator, a former Virginia Governor, DNC Chairman, Lieutenant Governor, Mayor of Richmond, and City Councilor, had a resume almost as expansive as Clinton's. As an added plus, Kaine was fluent in Spanish, completely respected by peers in both parties, and an avid harmonica instrumentalist. At his announcement rally in Miami, the folksy Kaine promised the crowd that he and Clinton would be "compañeros de alma" in the great "lucha" ahead. The Senator further noted that he shared the same creed as Hillary, to "do all the good you can".

The long-fought race for the Democratic nomination was over. The country's left-leaning electorate had decided which candidate they wanted to run against the Republican nominee. Bernie stayed in the race until the convention, seemingly standing by in case Hillary was indicted or further investigated for the email scandal that had plagued her campaign. Having spent months on the campaign trail and his dreams of becoming president emboldened by several primary victories, it was hard for Bernie to concede he had lost. After attempting to direct the platform committee and demanding a keynote address during the Primetime coverage of the DNC Convention, Bernie ultimately suspended his campaign and ended his bid for the White House. "I move that Hillary Clinton be selected as the nominee of the Democratic Party" Bernie Sanders asserted, calling for Clinton's nomination by acclamation. Sanders made the declaration during Vermont's vote at the culmination of the delegate roll call on the floor of the DNC Convention in Philadelphia.

After the roll call, Clinton addressed the convention via telecast, shattering a digital glass ceiling. She joined President Obama on stage the following day after he delivered a passionate endorsement of her campaign. Hillary's husband, daughter Chelsea, and the newly introduced Vice Presidential nominee Tim Kaine gave enthusiastic speeches, asking America to take the monumental leap...elect the first woman president and shatter the figurative glass ceiling in the process. On the final day, Hillary took the stage, impassioning young women and girls to dream big and follow their dreams. As the red, white, and blue balloons fell from the ceiling, Clinton and Kaine raised their interlocked hands, accepting the nomination of the Democratic Party for president and vice president.

CHAPTER FOUR: REPUBLICAN PRIMARY - LOW ENERGY JEB, LYIN' TED, AND LITTLE MARCO

From the beginning of the election season, an unclear date that seems to occur earlier each cycle, there appeared to be a favorite for the Republican Party's presidential nomination. Before any major candidates officially announced their intentions of running, a series of rumors anticipated what the lineup might look like. Former nominee Mitt Romney, who lost to Obama in 2012, would have been the clear frontrunner, but he declared the 2012 election his last. Next up on the shortlist was Romney's former running mate, Wisconsin Congressman Paul Ryan. Though Ryan seemed like a shoo-in for the 2016 nomination, he too wasn't interested, leaving the pool of candidates wide open. Instead, it was a Southern swing-state Governor who seemed the most likely candidate for the GOP nod, especially since his father and brother were former presidents and he himself had overwhelming support of party insiders.

Jeb Bush was a high-quality candidate for the presidency. Much like his brother George, Jeb had followed in his family's political footsteps, becoming the Governor of Florida in the wake of his father's presidency. Bush was married to a Mexican immigrant and had served as the successful Governor of a densely minority populated state – both excellent assets to swing the much-needed Latino vote away from the Democratic Party. In 2012, he had been rumored to be on the Romney campaign's shortlist for vice president. Hailing from a politically pivotal state, Jeb would make an unquestionable 2016 favorite in the electoral math.

On December 16, 2014, Bush created an exploratory committee for the presidential race, a usual first step for top-tier candidates seeking to garner public opinion and fundraise before formally getting into the race. Although numerous challengers and even the uncommitted Mitt Romney polled higher in national surveys than Bush, the former Florida Governor made it official on June 15, 2015, declaring his candidacy for President of the United States. He joined a growing pool of conservative candidates in a primary election that was sure to be unique.

Texas junior Senator Ted Cruz, who had announced his candidacy first, in March of 2015, was a favorite amongst the Tea Party conservatives. He made his presence known in the 2012 elections by disassociating himself from the establishment base of the Republican Party and preaching strict evangelical conservative views. Cruz was the early leader in the race – a position that would allow for strong fundraising and give his campaign energy that could last through the primaries. As an outspoken legislator, Cruz never shied away from a debate and was never one who cared about the opinions of his colleagues. While he had marginal support on "The Hill", he had a strong and growing base of Republicans nationwide who were "sick of the status quo."

Florida Senator Marco Rubio, the star-child of the Republican Party and a likely future candidate for president, joined Cruz in the race on April 13th. He jumped right in, so self-confident that he refused to run for reelection for his own U.S. Senate seat. His campaign theme declared the need for "a new American century". Rubio made the case that it was time for a fresh, young, and energetic conservative to lead the Republican Party. He had support across the party from minorities to young Republicans looking for a youthful candidate unburdened by years in the conservative establishment like previous nominees. Marco quickly became one of the leaders in the race for a place on the GOP ticket.

In addition to the political favorites, three outsiders entered the race. First was New York real estate mogul Donald Trump, followed by retired neurosurgeon Ben Carson and former Hewlett-Packard CEO Carly Fiorina. Carson argued that his time as the Director of Pediatric Neurosurgery for Johns Hopkins Hospital, in addition to the well-documented success of a surgery separating conjoined twins, demonstrated he had the leadership and critical thinking skills necessary to run the country. Fiorina, like Trump, was a business leader. She had led a large company through difficult times in America's economy and argued she could be the first female president of the United States, just as she was the first female CEO of a Fortune 20 company.

A host of other political candidates joined the field too, including Governors Christie, Gilmore, Huckabee, Jindal, Kasich, Pataki, Perry, and Walker. Senators Graham, Santorum, and Paul also dove into the campaign pool, making their cases that the next president (like Obama) could be a former U.S. Senator instead of a governor, businessman/woman, or a political foreigner. Each employed their own unique strategy to try to get attention from the media and build public support for their campaign.

Just from the sheer number of contenders, polls shifted wildly in the year leading up to the first Republican debate. As the large field was coming together and people began listening to the candidates on the trail, strength for early leaders waned and support for political newcomers grew. By September, it was quickly becoming clear that the Republican electorate was searching for a no-nonsense, non-mainstream, and non-establishment candidate that wasn't held back from speaking his/her mind nor bound by the need to be politically correct. Trump, Carson, Cruz, and Rubio began to make inroads on the polling advantage held by Governors Scott Walker of Wisconsin and Jeb Bush of Florida, with Trump ultimately leading the pack going into debate season.

The first debate of the Republican primary contest took place in Cleveland at the very stadium that months later would be home to the Republican National Convention. The candidates joined together on August 6th, 2015, to debate the issues and the controversial claims each had made on the campaign trail. Though seventeen candidates had declared, only the ten highest polling aspirants received a spot on the main stage. (Candidates polling under the top ten debated earlier at a non-Primetime hour, but on the same stage.) Moderated by the conservative-friendly Fox News, the debate brought in over 24 million viewers and set the record for the highest presidential primary debate and non-sport related cable viewership.

The candidates were lined up in order of their polling average. The favorites, Trump, Bush, and Walker were at center stage, flanked by the rest. Bret Baer, the host of *Special Report* on Fox News, caused a ruckus with his first question. He challenged the candidates, by a show of hands, asking who was unwilling to "pledge their support to the eventual nominee of the Republican Party and pledge to not run an independent campaign against that person." Silence abounded. Only one candidate raised his hand…Donald Trump.

Trump later argued that if he were the Republican nominee, he would pledge not to run as an independent, yet he would not promise to support any nominee other than himself. Immediately several of the other candidates suggested Trump was "hedging his bets on Hillary Clinton", arguing that The Donald was never a Republican in the first place and hadn't even stood for the GOP platform for most of his adult life. Thus began the tumultuous campaign – verbal attacks against Donald Trump followed by counter punches and preemptive strikes from the outspoken frontrunner. A bawdy barrage of retorts would become the new normal in a most unusual election.

Unlike the Democrat's Primary process, the GOP nominee selection procedure involves winning allocated delegates without superdelegates. A provision included in the RNC charter (Rule 9) allows the National Committee to "fill any vacancies" which might occur by reason of "death, declination, or otherwise." This ambiguous provision, which would become headline news in the 2016 election cycle, could feasibly have given the RNC the ability to pick a nominee other than one selected by the voters.

Even the most politically savvy consultants and campaign operatives have a hard time maneuvering the GOP primary rules. The instructions for delegate allocation are so mired with legalese only a handful of people can successfully explain them. Many contests are winner-takes-all, making the primary process shorter as candidates who lose a contest even by a small margin are not awarded delegates proportionately. Several states do award their delegates proportionately, especially in frontloaded early voting states, giving minor candidates a chance to get a share of delegates without winning. For the GOP, each state has its own system for delegate allocation with some using a strict winner-take-all, others using a triggered winner take all (if a candidate received the majority, they'd take all the delegates up for grabs), or some form of proportional allocation.

The plurality setup of the primary process does create a political quandary, however, where losing candidates can seat friendly national delegates at respective state conventions with hopes of flipping states at a contested convention. Most delegates are bound to vote on the first ballot at the national convention for the candidate who won their state, although there are uncommitted and RNC delegates that make up a fractional amount of the total delegate pool. Across 56 primaries and caucuses, with a total of 2,472 delegates, a candidate must win 1,237 delegates to achieve a plurality and become the party's presumptive nominee before the convention.

The Republican primary became the biggest name-calling and insult-driven contest on record. The candidates threw verbal punches and slights at their opponents on debate stages and at rallies across the country. Donald Trump gave each of his serious challengers a nickname, meant as insults, though often serving as a fundraising opportunity by both the denigrator and the candidate who was slandered. Senator Marco Rubio (being shorter than Trump) became "Little Marco", an attack meant to imply more than just a difference in "height" between the two candidates. The nickname might also have originated from the world's smallest water bottle that Rubio awkwardly sipped from during his Republican response to the State of the Union Address in 2013, or it could have been inspired from a photo of the Senator on a giant rocking chair published by *Drudge Report*. Senator Ted Cruz received the title "Lyin' Ted" (spelling and apostrophe defined by Trump at a rally in New York) after Trump accused Cruz of lying, Bible in hand, to the Senator's largely evangelical base.

Early on in the primary season, Trump nicknamed Governor Bush "Low Energy Jeb" after the governor's poll numbers started to fall. Jeb pushed back, replying to a lighthearted question during the 2nd GOP debate on CNN, suggesting his Secret Service code name would be "Eveready" – adding it's "high energy, Donald" (an answer that earned Jeb a high-five from the frontrunner). Not to be outdone, Trump postulated his Secret Service codename could be "Humble" (a response that won laughs from the crowd and Governor Bush for the irony). Lesser-used nicknames coined by Trump included "1 for 38" – later "1 for 41" (John Kasich's nickname after winning only the Ohio Primary), "Crazy Megyn" (Fox News anchor Megyn Kelly), "Low I.Q. Crazy Mika" (*Morning Joe* co-host Mika Brzezinski), "Psycho Joe" (*Morning Joe* co-host Joe Scarborough), and "Pocahontas" (Massachusetts Senator Elizabeth Warren).

Throughout the GOP primary campaign, numerous themes arose as the issues of discussion and dissention between the nomination hopefuls expanded. In classic conservative political fashion, national security and foreign policy were central to the platforms each campaign was laying out. Unlike most previous election years, the Republican candidates embraced a shift from political correctness towards honest, often insensitive and offensive, campaign rhetoric. Senators Paul and Cruz, businessman Trump, and Dr. Carson championed the effort to get away from scripted lines and focus groups, to attack their opponents and the left for concentrating on what people wanted to hear versus what the candidate thought they needed to hear. As usual, the size of the federal government, especially the oversight and reach into social issues, was at the heart of the conservative interchange during the primary contest.

When Donald Trump announced his candidacy for president, he spoke about the influx of illegal immigrants from Mexico coming to the United States and the need for firm border security. Trump hit a nerve in the country by bringing up a controversial issue that while often not openly discussed was in the minds of the conservative electorate. Trump suggested that the Mexican government was "smarter and much more cunning" than the American leaders Donald deemed "stupid". At campaign rallies in Border States and across the American South, Trump built up animosity toward the Obama Administration's acceptance of illegal immigrants, deceitfully suggesting the White House was giving them amnesty. Donald promised that he would deport the illegal immigrants. Other candidates argued that illegals that had lived in America for their entire lives (Dreamers) deserved a path to earned legal status, although amnesty was off the table.

Trump also called for the creation of a massive border wall, one he claimed he could negotiate Mexico to pay for. Trump blamed the failed border fence and lack of patrol agents for the huge illegal immigration in America, suggesting that Mexicans could easily just walk across the border. Senator Rubio pointed out that most illegal entrants to America came from Latin America instead of Mexico, with Kasich arguing that while Trump was onto something, he (Kasich) and the rest of the candidates had different solutions. Rubio was Trump's primary challenger on "the wall" advising Trump of its subterranean limitations, noting that a motivated individual could simply tunnel under a multi-billion dollar wall defeating the purpose altogether. Later, Trump would be a faultfinder on his border wall pointing out that if an illegal immigrant managed to climb the wall, there might be a simple way down. During a rally in New Hampshire, Trump argued, "Once they get up there, there will be no way to get down. Well, maybe a rope, but..." More than one commentator suggested he was implying lynching instead of repelling down the face of the wall.

In addition to border related issues, the debates and campaign trail rallies focused on the need to address domestic threats including "Sanctuary Cities". All of the candidates condemned the use of local illegal immigrant protections, a practice used for decades by liberal cities to shield people without legal status from federal prosecution and expulsion. Conservatives have fulminated against the practice, especially after the shooting of 32-year-old Kathryn (Kate) Steinle on the San Francisco Embarcadero in 2015 by a five-time deportee originally from Guanajuato, Mexico. Cruz won support across the country and moved into second place after defending his adamant position against Sanctuary Cities. He sponsored a vote in the Senate on the Kate's Law Act, a revision to the Immigration and Nationality Act of 1965, which would end such programs.

The Islamic State of Iraq and the Levant (ISIL) and terrorism were major points of agreement between the broad field of candidates. Each promised to protect America, defeat ISIL (ISIS), and use the term "Radical Islamic Terrorism", a phrase they felt the Obama/Clinton Democrats should use to describe ISIL. Senator Rand Paul called for the end of arms sales to ISIL aligned countries. Cruz promised to carpet bomb ISIL targets suggesting his administration would "see if sand glows in the dark". Each also pledged to renegotiate or at least take a new look at the Joint Comprehensive Plan of Action (Iran Nuclear Deal). Consensus among the candidates that Iran was dishonest and was a state sponsor of terrorism drove the conversation to a regional reorganization, changing Obama foreign policy in the Middle East from nation-building and international aid to a dizzying mix of containment and isolationism.

On domestic issues, an area where Republicans are generally weaker than national security, all of the candidates called for a reduction in the size of government, most arguing for cutting departments like Commerce, Energy, Education, and the Internal Revenue Service. They called for an end to the Common-Core education strategy, Planned Parenthood funding, and the repeal and replacement of the landmark Patient Protection and Affordable Care Act, affectionately named Obamacare. Abortion and pro-life objection to women's reproductive rights as well as opposition to marriage equality was showcased on debate stages and at campaign events across the country. Only Gov. Kasich said he was willing to defend marriage equality recognizing, "just because someone doesn't think the way I do, doesn't mean I can't care about them or love them." "That's what we are taught when we have strong faith", he reminded the others.

One core imbroglio loomed in the failure of Donald Trump to release his federal tax returns. Unlike every major candidate for president before him since Richard Nixon (with the exception of Gerald Ford), Trump didn't release his tax returns. The practice, although not part of election law, was customary of all major party contenders as a way of showing the American electorate that they are not beholden to any foreign governments. By withholding his IRS filings, Trump managed to cover up the extent to which his personal and business dealings were tied to foreign investors and corrupt governments outside the United States – an important piece of a puzzle still being solved on foreign involvement in America's elections. Both his Republican and Democratic challengers called out the New York businessman and "alleged" billionaire for his refusal to submit even an antiquated tax return. A secondary possibility for Trump's decision not to release his tax returns and instead claim they were under an IRS audit could have been his failure to pay federal taxes. A filing made public that included a few pages of Trump's 1995 tax returns suggested he had paid little to no federal income taxes for decades – even as he recognized earnings in the tens of millions of dollars.

If Trump had not paid taxes since the 1990s, he hadn't paid for the government programs his administration would lead if he won...including the U.S. military. At least these were the arguments that the Cruz, Rubio, Clinton, and Sanders campaigns made. Nearly every American news outlet featured a discussion on Trump's taxes and the contributions he may or may not have made to the American government he was campaigning to lead.

The racial divide in America that made inroads in the Democratic nominee selection process also carried weight on the right. Donald Trump condemned multilingual candidates for giving speeches in Spanish, advocating support for making English the national language and restarting the English-Only Movement. Trump also made clear his admonition of allowing languages other than "American" to be used or even allowed by the government. He suggested only allowing immigrants into America if they speak English fluently, even though by law, the United States has no official language. Although American English is the lingua franca of the melting pot that Trump was campaigning to govern, he had little solid footing to demand it be the sole language allowed. Trump himself appeared linguistically challenged when it came to American English…even though he argued, "I know words. I have the best words." One needn't look further than his tweets on Twitter to realize diction and writing were not strengths of the GOP candidate turned Republican nominee. Nor was his articulation any better, as evident during rally speech deliveries or epigrammatic arguments at debates.

The frontrunner also called for a ban of Muslims traveling to the United States and ending the birthright citizenship clause. His plan for a "Muslim Ban" would later be retooled to focus on the threat of what Trump called "Radical Islamic Terrorism", a shift that prompted the policy to be renamed "Extreme Vetting". Carson, the only African American candidate in the field on either side of the political spectrum, attempted to end the racial tension at a debate specifying, "A neurosurgeon operates on the thing that makes people who they are. Skin and hair don't make people who they are…time to move beyond that. Strength comes from unity."

Each of the conservatives vying for the nomination had their own view of what America should look like and how the country would be different if they were president. For most, the desire to fix what they saw was wrong with the federal bureaucracy, usually related to the size of government and the way the Obama Administration was leading, drove their consideration to run for Obama's replacement. Pundits indicated that for Donald Trump it was personal. Aside from his ego and a desire to hold America's most prominent office in the spotlight of the international media,

Trump had a personal vendetta against the scoffs that joked about his possible contention for the presidency. It has been argued that Trump's presidential run stemmed from the attacks by President Obama and comedians at several White House Correspondents Dinners. Many believe that continuous personal blows by the President, in response to Trump's advocacy of the birther movement along with his flamboyant and extravagant personality, resolved the wealthy businessman to consider unseating the Obama Democratic stranglehold on the Oval Office.

In 2015 before the first delegates were awarded, Governors Jindal, Pataki, Perry, and Walker along with Senator Lindsay Graham withdrew from contention...although their names remained on some ballots. On February 1st, Senator Ted Cruz won the Iowa Caucus with 27.6 percent of the vote, taking 8 delegates to Trump's 7; Rubio, Carson, Bush, Fiorina, Huckabee, Kasich, and Paul split the remaining 14 delegates. Poor performances in Iowa saw Huckabee, Santorum, and Paul drop out before New Hampshire. Trump won that state, plus two other early contests (South Carolina and Nevada), and took a heavy delegate lead. Christie, Fiorina, and Gilmore dropped out after New Hampshire; Bush threw in the towel after South Carolina.

Super Tuesday in March of 2016 added clarification to the race by anointing Trump as the clear favorite winning 7 of the 11 states up for grabs. Cruz took three states (Alaska, Oklahoma, and his home state of Texas), Rubio won in Minnesota, and Ben Carson suspended his campaign after a poor showing, winning only 3 delegates. With Carson's departure, only Trump, Cruz, Rubio, and Kasich were left. Win after win; Trump began to separate from the pack. Cruz and Rubio teamed up to attack, hoping to end Trump's early momentum and gain ground for themselves. Rubio also tried to bolster the Ohio Governor by asking his supporters to turn out for Kasich in Ohio, thus hoping Kasich voters would support Rubio in Florida. That plan ultimately failed, causing Rubio to concede his home state to Trump and suspend his campaign.

Cruz and Kasich later teamed up to take on Trump in a crafty nonaggression political pact. Cruz backed off Oregon and New Mexico so as not to compete with Kasich, who backed off Indiana. Ultimately, Trump won all three. Even though Trump held a majority of delegates and Cruz and Kasich had no mathematical road to a nomination, the two continued. They hoped to prevent Trump from getting enough delegates to win before the convention. Had their attempt been successful, a contested convention could have thrown the nomination to Cruz, Kasich, or another conservative through the manipulation of national convention candidates by selective state convention electioneering or RNC-Rule 9. Cruz had already seated national delegates in numerous states that would have flipped on a second or successive ballot to support him if Trump received a plurality instead of an outright majority of delegates. After a Trump victory in Indiana, Cruz and Kasich both suspended their campaigns, remaining on the ballot in the final state primaries but preventing a floor fight at the convention.

Donald Trump picked Indiana Governor Mike Pence to be his running mate, citing the Hoosier's executive experience and strong conservative stance. (According to campaign insiders, Pence joined New Jersey Governor Chris Christie and former Speaker of the House Newt Gingrich on Trump's shortlist for his running mate.) Establishment Republicans lauded the selection of Pence who was empirically the most conservative Vice Presidential pick in over fifty years. Pence told the press he would play a substantial role in a Trump presidency, pledging to serve as an advisor to Trump much like VP Dick Cheney had to President George W. Bush in the early 2000s.

The Republican primary process wasn't without its blunders and interesting political deceptions. At the ABC News sponsored debate, Trump, Carson, and Kasich stayed backstage when the moderators blundered the candidate announcement to a hyped and loud crowd (they eventually came out when the moderators announced the candidate's names to a toned down audience). Cruz, in an attempt to build support for his campaign, announced a Vice Presidential pick in Carly Fiorina at a campaign rally. He also tried to capitalize on an erroneous CNN tweet by suggesting Carson was taking a break from the campaign. (The Cruz campaign sent an email to their volunteers before the New Hampshire Primary urging them to tell voters Carson had dropped out and urging Granite Staters to vote for Cruz instead of wasting a vote on a candidate no longer in the race.) Even the release of the Trump-Pence campaign logo ahead of the RNC Convention created disturbance. The questionable symbol was supposed to pair the letters T for Trump and P for Pence in the canton of an American flag using the styling of a baseball team emblem. Unfortunately, the tip of the descending "T" protruded through the center of the "P" in a manner reminiscent of a common high school hand gesture insinuating sexual intercourse. Posts on social media compared the TP to toilet paper and the stripes on the flag to a barcode on a bag of Cheetos (a slight at Trump's complexion and notorious burnt-orange hair). Pundits took it a step further, teasing the logo as a coital embrace of Trump by Pence (poking fun at Pence's conservative roots and staunch stance on homosexuality).

Trump, the presumptive candidate, went into the National

Convention with the record for Republican Primary votes at 14,015,993. Together Cruz, Kasich, and Rubio received over 15 million votes – meaning most Republican voters didn't vote for the eventual nominee, instead a record-breaking majority voted against the New York businessman. The GOP Convention in Cleveland, Ohio (Kasich's home state) was divisive. Most prominent Republicans had endorsed Trump either during or immediately after the primary process, yet several key figures refused to give their support. The entire Bush family (including the 41st and 43rd Presidents), Governor Kasich, Senator Cruz, and former GOP nominee Mitt Romney refused to endorse the nominee on or after May 3rd, when Trump met the required delegate count to secure the nomination. During a surprising address to the convention, Cruz encouraged RNC delegates to "vote their conscience". Nevertheless, Trump became the Republican Party's formal nominee on July 19th, 2016, when Alabama Senator Jeff Sessions nominated him on the convention floor. The roll call of states secured a win with the lowest delegate count since the 1976 RNC convention.

CHAPTER FIVE: THE PRESIDENTIAL CAMPAIGN FROM HELL

The 2016 election has been described as vitriolic and nasty, divisive and polarizing, raw and demagogic, even emotionally energizing. Each side threw powerful punches, called the other out for moral indiscretions, and lodged character assaults right and left. The disgust for the right by those on the left was only outweighed by the distrust for the left by the political right. It was, by far, a campaign from hell.

Starting out as a nasty campaign, it grew worse – filled with anger, politically charged attacks, and sexist odium. The Republicans reveled at the chance to unseat the Obama/Clinton machine that conservative media had blamed for every problem in American history since the 1990s. The Democrats were energized to elect the first female president of the United States, continuing the progress made under the Obama Administration. Both sides were doubled down in advocacy for their respective agendas, believing they had the best solutions to tackle the new challenges America would face. Neither side was interested in working together in a bipartisan approach to policy or political leadership. Clinton's campaign did hope to unite the divided country after the election, expecting to work with Republicans as the former Secretary had during her tenure at the State Department and in the United States Senate. On the right, disgusting insults had become a part of the political process; the party's nominee calling his opponents, the media, and anyone who challenged him offensive slurs.

The War on Women

The Clinton campaign communications staff expertly outlined Trump's previous assertions of women, bringing to light the GOP candidate's words verbatim on female leaders in business, media, and politics. Throughout his life and continuing through the campaign, Donald Trump degraded women, publicly calling them pigs, slobs and dogs. He suggested that pregnancy wasn't good for employers, implied women weren't capable of doing as good a job as men, and humiliated women whom he found unattractive. He disgraced talk show hosts and debate moderators for asking him tough questions, once saying of Fox News (*Kelly File*) host Megyn Kelly, "you could see there was blood coming out of her eyes, blood coming out of her wherever."

Sexism in America is real, and the Clinton campaign rightfully jumped on the issue. Treating women equal to men isn't a wedge issue, it's not a political issue, but it's constitutionally expected and morally decent. Women make up a majority of the electorate, yet outside of a few national campaigns, gender equity rarely makes the cut in a stump speech, let alone a presidential debate. When it did, who would have expected the reaction by the Republican right to be any different than it was in 2016 with Donald J. Trump at the helm of the party? After all, he was running against the first female to lead a major political party in a General Election in American history.

Hillary Clinton had always been a strong woman, very proud of what she has accomplished in her political, professional, and personal life. Her gender has been central to her success and her challenges in the political sector. For years she fought for equal standing. In 2016 she got it. After 240 years, America nominated a woman to lead a major party and go head to head with a man known to demean and degrade women. She faced numerous standards unparalleled of male candidates – but nevertheless, she persisted!

Optics

The 2016 presidential election was optics driven, a continuation of a growing political separation between Democrat and Republican strategies for handling the press and social media. The Trump campaign wanted the perception as an anti-elitist effort, whereas the Clinton camp played the mainstream card in choosing to run a more conventional campaign. Trump built a team of political outsiders relying heavily on his family who had little political experience. The Clinton campaign was organized around the best minds in Democratic Party politics, using former 2008 campaign and Obama Administration advisors as the backbone of their staff. Trump's team was largely older lobbyists and military advisors, whereas the younger, more energetic and experienced policy wonks flocked to support the Democratic nominee.

Energy was split between the two campaigns. The Clinton machine was able to excite many younger and first time voters, although her tough primary against democratic socialist Bernie Sanders made it difficult to pull onetime opponents into the fold. She especially inspired women and girls to hit the streets and campaign for her, most recognizing Clinton was the best chance for a female President of the United States in their lifetimes. On the right, Trump excited a new segment of the conservative base, bringing out thousands of older Americans who had taken a break from politics, but wanted their voices heard through the GOP candidate. While the levels of energy were different, unlike the 2008 and 2012 campaigns, the Republican candidate was able to spark a fire among the GOP electorate.

The Trump team scheduled large assemblies, propaganda events more analogous to the Nuremberg Rallies than a presidential campaign whistle-stop. The Shakespearianesque gatherings saw the candidate defend his positions on issues while debasing his opposition with unmatched nihilism for the American political process. Trump built a core base of passionate supporters, calling them to help "drain the swamp" and overturn the establishment conservative elites whom he blamed for inaction under the Obama presidency.

The Trump team took advantage of their candidate's passion and ability to hold the attention of an audience. When he didn't have a clear answer, Trump was encouraged to play to the party's base, attacking Democrats on key issues like national security, terrorism, and tax rates. Domestic and social issues not being strong areas for Trump, he spun to his strengths, igniting the base with fear. When he didn't have a response to the opioid crisis, he blamed minority communities. From education to trade, international relations to healthcare, Trump deflected when he lacked a good answer. Instead of challenging Democrats on their stance on social issues, Trump deferred to ISIL, border security, and job loss. During one rally speech Trump even insinuated that President Obama and Hillary Clinton started ISIL, "President Obama

– is the founder of ISIS – he founded ISIS – and I would say the cofounder would be crooked Hillary Clinton". Unfortunately for Clinton, many conservative voters accepted Trump's outlandish claim and further cemented their support for the Republican, ridiculous insinuations and all.

The Clinton camp took an approach opposite the Imperialistic, clenched-fist-waving attitude that was becoming commonplace at their challenger's events. Hillary spent hours meeting and listening to the people, holding coffee chats with municipal government officials, lunches with business leaders, and a slice of New York's finest (pizza) with families. She held much smaller campaign rallies, opting to spend her time on the trail at more intimate events. Her campaign favorite was the town hall forum that allowed voters to ask questions, raise concerns, and hear her direct responses.

Press and Media

The 2016 campaign will no doubt be remembered for the ugly relationship between politics and the media. After the 24-hour news cycle parsed every word of the candidates in the primaries, both General Election campaigns recognized the need to carefully tiptoe around their traveling press corps and the larger media establishment. Each communications cohort acknowledged that journalists and reporters were monitoring their candidate's every move – their every word. Trump took the constant coverage of his rallies and deconstruction of the words in each speech as an attack by what he deemed a liberal-biased "mainstream media".

While arguably both candidates had their fair share of superfluous media scrutiny, Trump was the only one who blasted the legitimacy of the free press...one that had the audacity to print, replay, and post his words verbatim. He challenged the integrity of nearly every news outlet, regarding journalists who ran stories he disagreed with as propagators of the "Fake News". The GOP nominee even criticized the empirically nonpartisan *New York Times* and *Wall Street Journal* – two papers that had historically been very fair to Republicans. Although Trump despised the media, his team appreciated the free coverage and capitalized on the attention for political gain even though they didn't value the press as an essential element of civil society. Donald detested being fact-checked by the media but loved having his interviews streamed nationwide.

The Trump campaign made numerous press avails, whereas Clinton was actively shielded from the media, focusing attention on the individual voters instead. Donald Trump's strategy from the start was to overwhelm the media, providing as many interviews as he could fit in his schedule. Unlike Clinton who was more reserved, Trump was cavalier in interviews and TV appearances, failing to hold back. Previous elections had been composed of candidates who filtered their speech for political correctness...not Trump. Instead, he relished in exciting news anchors and journalists with off-the-cuff remarks frequented with insults.

The Trump campaign took advantage of their candidate's celebrity and unfiltered, often undignified rhetoric to lock down near constant interviews. Trump claimed his free media and appearances on "the shows" gave him the upper hand, speaking directly to the American people without the focus groups and political correctness his opponent leaned on in crafting a consistent, relevant, and optimistic message with confident intellect. There was a clear correlation between Trump's proclivity to answer directly to the press and his position in the polls. Voters responded to the candidate's frankness however insulting and damaging the vernacular.

As a candidate, Clinton had always been more standoffish with the media. The press had caused her stress in the 2008 campaign against the natural smooth-talking Obama who could easily navigate targeted cross-examination by the media. In the 2016 cycle, her campaign made an effort to limit her direct interaction with reporters, choosing to give the press audience to Clinton's one-on-one interactions with the American people instead of candidate-focused gaggles. She was often branded as duplicitous for her controlled appearances at media avails. The Clinton campaign recognized they could stay on message better with their candidate connecting with the people. The communications staff shared the daily tick-tock in briefings to the campaign's traveling press corps. Nevertheless, Secretary Clinton made several in-person and phone-in, one-on-one interviews with journalists, reporters, bloggers, 'vloggers', podcasters, cable news correspondents, and TV cohosts. The Democratic candidate also held frequent public speeches and policy addresses, providing the media with campaign insight beyond regular events and briefings.

The Trump campaign was a breath of fresh air to the largely complacent GOP electorate. Passion had been lacking in the party since Reagan; few saw any of the political insiders in Washington as inspirational figures. For many, Donald Trump was everything that the party had not been since the 1980s. He provided a PC-filter free narrative for the problems America faced and a broad-brush, "Make America Great Again" approach to repairing the country they saw as wrecked by Obama-supporting egalitarians. Trump's campaign had a unique charisma that encouraged his base of generally non-college-educated white voters that the system was broken...Trump alone could fix it.

In contrast, Clinton's campaign was antiseptic, lacking the sex appeal of Obama's 2008 legendary rise. In 2016, the Democratic strategy was experience, emphasizing steady leadership and diplomatic solutions while exercising caution instead of taking risks. Clinton inspired millions – especially females, the educated, and minorities, however, she lacked the magnetism and star power that brought hundreds of thousands to Obama rallies eight years before. Unlike President Obama, who was seen around the world as the savior of the American promise (a change to believe in), Clinton was a continuation of the status quo, a third term of Obama or a second go-around of her husband's presidency.

Debauchery

Numerous questions and responses during the debates incorporated Trump's foul language from the past and present. The first question of the Second Presidential Debate specifically addressed the vulgar language and Trump's disgusting behavior before the debate. Patrice Brock asked the candidates, "The last presidential debate could have been rated as TV/MA, (mature audiences) per TV parental guidelines. Knowing that educators assign viewing the presidential debates as students' homework, do you feel you are modeling appropriate and positive behavior for today's youth?" It was a fantastic opening question for Secretary Clinton, one that clearly was pointed at her opponent on her political and literal right. Hillary responded saying she wanted a campaign of issues, not one of insults.

Regrettably, the 2016 campaign was never really about a wide variety of issues affecting the American people, at least not on one side. The diplomatic relationship between Secretary Clinton and

Donald Trump degraded quickly with insults thrown from the right and big vocabulary projected from the left. Donald Trump took every opportunity he could to insult his way to the top of the Republican Primary. After his coronation at the RNC Convention in Cleveland, he continued to go after anyone that stood in his way. While the Clinton family was the target of choice, Trump didn't forget to insult others on his climb into the presidential history books. He aimed at anyone who seemed to delegitimize his campaign or who questioned his ability or intelligence. Although it could be argued that those attacks against Trump weren't baseless, his counterstrikes against women, veterans, minorities, and other politicians were.

At the 2016 DNC convention, a Gold Star family (parents of a fallen U.S. Soldier) came on stage in support of Hillary Clinton and to criticize Trump's hateful policy towards Muslims. Khizr Kahn, the father of U.S. Army Captain Humayun Khan (who died fighting in Iraq) asked if Trump had ever read the American Constitution, offering to lend the GOP nominee his personal copy. Later, Trump would fire back, attacking the Gold Star family and the memory of their son's heroic service to the United States. Trump doubled down on his disregard for Captain Kahn's family at the 2nd Presidential Debate. He unbelievably stated, "If I were president at the time, he (Captain Khan) would still be alive." While establishment Republicans in Congress admonished Trump's rhetoric, Trump supporters didn't mind the negative remarks directed to a veteran's family. The ISIL online magazine Dabiq jumped on the scandal, using Trump's precise words as they had several times throughout the election to inspire their base and encourage the radicalization of new recruits.

Trump's attacks on veterans weren't limited to Gold Star Families; he went after one of the most respected American servicemen in the country, Arizona's senior U.S. Senator John McCain. During the primaries, Trump attended the Family Leadership Summit in Ames, Iowa, where he said of McCain, "He's not a war hero. He was a war hero because he was captured. I like people who weren't captured." Regardless of his political beliefs, Senator McCain has dedicated most of his life to serving his country, both in the military and in politics. He is a straight shooter, respected on both sides of the aisle, a moderate politician, and most certainly an American hero!

It is physically impossible to list all of the egregious actions and behaviors of the GOP candidate during and before the 2016 election. They are simply too numerous and frankly too disgusting. Yet it would be remiss not to also mention Mr. Trump's rhetoric regarding minorities and people with disabilities. In June of 2016, Trump condemned a federal judge who was presiding over a lawsuit against Donald's failed fraudulent education scheme Trump University. The GOP candidate suggested that since Judge Gonzalo Curiel was Hispanic, he would be biased against Trump who had earlier claimed Mexicans were "rapists and criminals" and had called for the construction of the largest border barricade in the world. (Curiel was born in Indiana, is an American citizen, the son of naturalized American citizens, and was appointed to the California Superior Court by Republican Governor Schwarzenegger.)

Trump also suggested that immediately after the September 11th terrorist attacks on the Twin Towers in New York City, Muslims across the tri-state area were rejoicing the implosion of the World Trade Center. During an interview with ABC's George Stephanopoulos, Trump stated he had witnessed, "people cheering on the other side of New Jersey, where you have large Arab populations...they were cheering as the World Trade Center came down." In response to a newspaper article discussing Trump's unsubstantiated claim of Muslims cheering after 9/11, the candidate mocked a reporter who had debunked the bogus and bigoted claim. At a campaign rally, Trump imitated Serge Kovaleski, a *New York Times* reporter who has arthrogryposis that causes joint contracture. The GOP candidate ridiculed Kovaleski by shaking and flailing his arms while yelling, "You've got to see this guy, Uhh, I don't know what I said...uhh, I don't remember, he's going like, I don't remember...maybe that's what I said."

Common at Trump rallies was the chant, "Lock Her Up!" The recitation was in reference to Clinton's email scandal and unjustified responsibility for the deadly attack on the American diplomatic outpost in Benghazi, Libya. When Trump would attack Clinton's experience, the crowd would break out into loud, erratic chants of "Lock Her Up!" Trump went through patterns of joining in and condemning the repetitions throughout the race, often choosing the former. Even at the RNC Convention, one of his staunch supporters former Lt. General Mike Flynn led the crowd in calls to "Lock Her Up!"

In response to Trump's remarks, Clinton often fought back by supporting her opponent's targets and using her advanced vocabulary to craft intellectual retorts to his divisive rhetoric. She did call out her opponent directly, suggesting that half of his supporters constituted a "basket of deplorables", a talking point she later would walk back. At a Presidential Debate, Clinton confirmed her argument wasn't "with his supporters"...it was "with him." Nevertheless, she usually refrained from getting caught in the mess, choosing to take the proverbial high road and stay focused on the issues. Recognizing Trump's dislike for the Obamas, Clinton frequently quoted First Lady Michelle Obama's catchphrase from the DNC convention in replies to Trump's statements, "When they (the GOP) go low, we (the Dems) go high!"

Besides disgusting and crass, the 2016 campaign for president will go down in history as the most divisive and downright undemocratic election cycle of modern times. Not only did Donald Trump alienate half of the American population and a greater portion of the rest of the world, he brought sex and lies to center stage. In a late primary season debate when Trump had already all but secured the nomination, he defended the size of his manhood. In response to a quip directed by Marco Rubio against Trump's small hands, the businessman retorted there was "no problem" with the size of his hands. He continued Rubio's suggestion that, "if they're small, something else must be small, I guarantee you there's no problem...I guarantee." In addition to discussing the size of his genitalia on stage, Trump also suggested during the primary that his other opponent's (Ted Cruz) father was an accomplice in the assassination of President John F. Kennedy.

Throughout the entire electoral progression, Trump continued to make vulgar remarks, perpetuate ridiculous rumors, and attack Secretary Clinton on his political left. He worked tirelessly to pit the former Secretary against Bernie Sanders' supporters, hoping to flip some millennials from the "Feel the Bern" column to the "Make America Great Again" team. Although many were disgusted with Trump's behaviors, his base was pleased to have a candidate not constrained by political correctness or afraid of contention. Even many Bernie Sanders supporters eventually found themselves in the Trump camp despite a negligible effort by the Senator to encourage his voters to back Clinton.

The Mommy and Daddy Problem in American Politics

The 2016 campaign had more than just an optics problem and a clear bully as the GOP bellwether. Like every presidential contest before it, at least in modern political history, the 2016 contest had a clear split in the rationale of the electorate to vote for a Democrat or Republican candidate. The NBC television show *The West Wing* called it the "Mommy Problem" when voters lean towards liberals for social change and conservatives for strength. When the country is searching for military strength and a Commander-in-Chief to tackle issues like national security and defense, they vote for a "Daddy" candidate. If the country is focused on domestic issues like education, healthcare, and infrastructure, they vote for the "Mommy" candidate. NBC's writing team hit the nail on the head with their analogy, just ask any political wonk and they'll tell you the same thing. Voters look for key strengths in candidates, aspects they think are most important for the country at that time in history.

Before Obama's Democratic Party victory in 2008, the economy, high unemployment numbers, and healthcare were top issues and the electorate pursued someone to fix them. Obama was the "Mommy" candidate offering a "Change We Can Believe In" strategy to tackle the social concerns that were responsible for the collapsing financial system. Eight years later, America's economy had seen years of growth and a record of continued job creation. Unlike 2008, there wasn't a major housing market crash or a crippling economic recession on the horizon. Instead in 2016, security was the major concern – especially after several mass shootings and domestic terror attacks across the country began to mimic the threats of ISIL occurring overseas. During the Obama years, healthcare had been solved for many Americans, particularly those who before the Affordable Care Act were without medical insurance coverage. Education was improving, and the federal government was making strides towards college affordability and student loan refinancing. Domestic issues were, by and large, better than eight years before when Obama took control of the White House. America appeared to need a "Daddy" more than a "Mommy" to lead the country forward.

Democrats can't generally beat Republicans on issues like border security, the threat of terrorism, nuclear proliferation, or national defense. So after security incidents nationwide, 2016 became the perfect storm for conservatives much like how 2008 was for liberals. It's because of the "Mommy/Daddy Problem" that three terms of party control over the White House is rare. After spending four years on an issue there is still likely room to improve, but after eight years it's harder to get support for the party to govern longer. Voters can't always see the accomplishments of the incumbent president's administration, a challenge that makes it appear that defense in Democratic governments or domestic issues in Republican administrations are being overlooked. In 2016, voters saw the threat of foreign-born terrorism and the need for increased national security and defense bolstering as priorities over furthering and building on the Obama Administration policies that had been the focus for the previous eight years.

On the Issues

It was bizarre watching the success of Donald Trump, a man with basically no political, public service, or educational background, campaign for the highest office in the country. After all, you wouldn't pick an airplane pilot by walking up to someone in an airport and asking him if he had ever flown a plane before...then inviting him to sit in the left seat of the cockpit when he's never even had a flight training class. Nor would you want a visitor in a hospital lobby to perform open-heart surgery. In practicality, it doesn't make sense to seat a man as president who's never served anyone but himself. A good occupant of the Oval Office needs to be familiar with the players, needs to know how to work with others – even across the aisle – and how to act presidential. Trump was a novice in politics and international relations. He'd negotiated real estate deals, but never socio-economic compacts; he'd made concessions in personal business contracts, but had no background leading peace talks or brokering conflict-ending treaties.

The successful septuagenarian businessman just didn't have the policy chops or political experience to make for an effective presidential leader. Unlike her opponent, Secretary Clinton had a broad understanding of both domestic issues and foreign policy implications on U.S. national security. Where she struggled was with the trivia frivolity of American politics. After decades in the national spotlight with scrutiny of her every move by the media and her political nemeses, Clinton had a baggage of rumors and potential scandals looming over her from the outset of her campaign. Trump couldn't defend his inexperience, so he attacked her on these almost daily. Donald quickly realized he could focus the national discussion on Clinton's emails, family indiscretions, and scrutinized political record instead of his naiveté and personal background of questionable behaviors. After all, the minutiae of a scandal always leads better on a television chyron than a platitude about experience or a slice of a leader's resume.

Most national campaigns focus on the needs of the country, the platforms of the candidates, and how to make their itineraries of change materialize. In 2016, the presidential contest was encumbered by scandals, surprises, and sexual allegations – far worse than the laughable use of a helmet while riding a tank that had trivialized a previous election (Dukakis in 1988). One candidate was the prepared student of history, equipped with a detailed answer, always ready to raise her hand, and supported by an expansive vocabulary...the other was Donald Trump. Unlike Clinton who had years of political know-how, Trump was learning on the road, usually breaking the rules at every turn and refusing to play by the book for running in a presidential election while standing centerfield on the national stage.

The Clinton machine (the candidate, her staff, and surrogates) had decades of practice serving in elected and appointed roles. They contributed a lifetime of national campaign knowledge. No one spoke for the Clinton camp that hadn't already prepared a clear and concise answer; everyone knew how to spin a story or pivot to his or her candidate's strengths. On the other side, Trump's team was basically new to politics. Outside of a few party insiders, Republican strategists, and pollsters, most of his staff was working on a national election for the first time, joining the candidate in making it up as they went. As a result, stories on the right often conflicted with the candidate himself, the party's position, or what Trump had just tweeted minutes earlier.

Twenty-five years in national politics, a lifetime in service, and a law degree gave Clinton incredible insight on how to run a campaign. She picked the best staff in the party, borrowing from the Obama campaign/White House to supplement her team from 2008. She crafted an intelligent message that clearly laid out her position on issues she knew were important to the American voter. Trump's business chops gave him a minor advantage on some economic questions, although he proved to be weak on taxes, the American economy, and job growth in the debates towards the end of the election – perhaps too late for anyone to notice.

Clinton had a definitive plan on how she was going to make America Stronger Together. Beyond a simple outline, she had a playbook that sketched a clear framework, point by point, on how she would work with lawmakers to move the country forward as a team. Stronger Together was more than just a talking point; it was a blueprint for bipartisan cooperation that would guide her extensive policies through Congress. She believed the country deserved more than empty platitudes and meaningless tautologies. America needed a plan of action with attainable goals and feasible cross-party collaboration. Her plan comprised volumes of studied policy, backed by science, statistics, and facts. It was completely paid for with every penny itemized for total transparency and each figure endorsed by the nation's leading economists.

Trump, on the other hand, had a less developed proposal. When asked about his campaign's platform, Trump had an ingenuous outline. Elect Trump and he would single-handedly Make America Great Again. Done! How would he do it? Easy...he'd first be elected and then he would simply Make America Great Again. Just don't ask him for further specifics about his plan or when America was last great. Donald's go to apothegm – Make America Great Again – also doubled as his campaign slogan, preventing the easily distracted businessman from needing to memorize a lengthy stump speech. His whole campaign platform could be shared in a single tweet with a few of the 140 characters left unused...leaving room to berate "Crooked Hillary", "Fake News", or the "Liberal Media".

The Ironies on the Election Trail

The General Election campaign was not without irony. On numerous occasions, Trump suggested that no one was more respectful to women than he was...a declaration he made twice while on stage with Secretary Clinton. Trump wanted to lock Hillary up for not allowing her emails to be made public, but ironically his tax returns couldn't be shown as full transparency on his part might jeopardize his audit. Throughout the whole campaign, he refused to publish his tax returns (a standard for presidential candidates) citing a federal audit as his rationale for retaining the records. On the other side, Clinton had released 39 years of returns.

The eccentric style of Mr. Trump's personality throughout the campaign was indicative of his infatuation with television drama. When Trump said, "I am the law and order candidate" at the RNC Convention, did he mean *Law and Order Special Victims Unit* or *Law and Order Criminal Intent*? It's as though American politics in 2016 was brought to us by NBC Universal and Dick Wolf...*Dun! Dun!*

Trump's campaign slogan "Make America Great Again" was positive enough, but his campaign theme music seemed much darker. At rallies across the country, he used the songs *It's The End Of The World*, by R.E.M, and the Rolling Stones classic, *You Can't Always Get What You Want*. The Clinton campaign chose Rachel Platten's *Fight Song*, Sara Bareilles' *Brave*, and *Stronger Together*, written by her campaign and performed by Jessica Sanchez as their official songs – more appropriate for a political operation of unity seeking to win a national election.

It's true that presidents need strong egos and a candidate needs an even bigger one. In order to gain the support of tens of millions of American voters, you have to have a high degree of confidence in yourself and an ability to sell yourself to the electorate. Many of the minor candidates in each party had failed at making a name for themselves in the race because they lacked the tenacity to go all in against the bigger names that flanked them on the debate stage. The "fired up, ready to go" after the frontrunner attitude, which ultimately gave Obama the win in 2008, was nowhere to be found in the 2016 primaries. Although ego is often considered to be a weakness, especially when it distracts you from seeing your success or diminishes the strength of a team, it is a necessary strength in politics. A robust self-image is an important characteristic of an effective politician; in 2016 two candidates with very different egos led their party's ticket.

There's a Cherokee legend that annotates the good and bad side of human self-centeredness that paints a picture of the difference between Trump and Clinton in 2016. As it goes, an aging Cherokee is explaining the intricacies of human life to his grandson saying, "A fight is going on inside me. It's a terrible fight and it's between two wolves. One is evil – he is anger, envy, sorrow, regret, greed, arrogance, self-pity, guilt, resentment, inferiority, lies, false pride, superiority, and ego. The other is good – he is joy, peace, love, hope, serenity, humility, kindness, benevolence, empathy, generosity, truth, compassion, and faith. The same fight is going on inside you – and inside every other person, too." According to the Cherokee parable, the grandson thinks about what his grandfather had said and then asks, "Which wolf will win?" The grandfather replies, "The one you feed." During the 2016 election, America was having that same fight...in the end one was fed more than the other.

Even though Donald Trump didn't meet the criteria of previous elections, namely experience and the "presidential look", he built incredible momentum and secured a sizeable base of staunch supporters. Trump grew up as a wealthy, overindulged prince, never having lived in the mainstream American life. In 2016, fame-starved and money-hungry postulants came out in force to support him. His celebrity quality put him on a pedestal; his narcissism perverted his mind into believing he could do no wrong and was superior to everyone. Trump's opposition of establishment politics boosted support amongst a faction of the American populace who felt left out and left behind by President Obama and his Democratic colleagues in Washington. His monomaniacal philosophy, rooted in extreme egocentricity, would have been unacceptable for anyone else, but for Trump it brought out crowds by the thousands. Pundits and scholars are still trying to understand how Trump managed to do what no other candidate, of either party, had done before.

Clinton too has a big ego, although her history of helping others and putting families and children first is unquestionable. While she was competing against a self-interested opponent, known for his blatant narcissism, she remained benevolent. Opportunities arose for her to go after Donald Trump, but she resisted until he attacked families, women, veterans, refugees, individuals with disabilities, and the disenfranchised. Even though she wanted a respectable campaign, above insults and attack ads, Clinton was forced to respond to the rhetoric from the other side. History will show that she criticized Trump on his inexperience, his hateful speech, his derogatory behavior, and the policies he supported. Where Trump launched assaults at Clinton personally, mostly predicated in rumor or outright lies, she responded by pushing back against one thing Trump didn't have going for him...facts!

CHAPTER SIX: THE OCTOBER SURPRISE – A BASKET OF DEPLORABLES ON A BUS

It happens every election cycle, an October Surprise upsets the race and occasionally flips support from the front-runner to their opponent. As far back as the 1964 presidential election, there has been a surprise media release or announcement in nearly every campaign for the White House. Numerous state and national campaign instances of so-called "October Surprises" have peppered American political history also. Due to the last minute occurrence of a newsbreak and with November elections on the horizon, an October Surprise often has a huge impact on a campaign's momentum and generally drives the narrative for the remaining days leading to the ballot box.

In 1972 during the Nixon/McGovern presidential contest, Henry Kissinger announced that the United States' effort negotiating the end of the Vietnam War was in sight. As the Nixon Administration's National Security Advisor and chief negotiator, Kissinger proclaimed that the administration believed peace was "at hand". The contentious conflict had played an expansive role in the American political conversation since the beginning of the U.S. involvement in the war. Stating "peace is at hand" gave the Nixon Campaign the extra energy it needed and depicted President Nixon as leading the effort to end American engrossment in the extremely unpopular and polarizing Vietnam War.

The Carter Administration and 1980 reelection campaign suffered from a negative October Surprise when the White House and the Iranian government both revealed that American hostages in the U.S. Embassy in Tehran wouldn't be released until after Election Day. While not necessarily responsible for Carter's crippling loss to Reagan on November 4th, 1980, the Iranian Hostage Crisis did have an impact on the race. Never confirmed to be involved in the eventual release of the hostages, the Reagan Campaign benefitted greatly by the announcement that the hostages would remain in Iran until after the U.S. elections took place. The American diplomats being held by student activists of the Muslim Student Followers of the Imam's Line were ultimately released to U.S. negotiators on January 20th, 1981, just moments after the conclusion of President Ronald Reagan's Inaugural Address on the steps of the U.S. Capitol.

News of the indictment of a Reagan Administration official in the Iran-Contra affair came to light in the summer before the 1992 election. Although the Iran-Contra political scandal didn't initially involve President George H.W. Bush, he was caught up in the ordeal having served as Vice President during the Reagan Administration. Lawrence Walsh, the Independent Counsel investigating Iran-Contra, was heavily criticized for bringing an indictment in the months leading up to the culmination of the 1992 presidential election. While the June '92 indictment of Reagan's Secretary of Defense Caspar Weinberger didn't technically materialize in October, its negative impact on the Bush campaign lasted through Election Day.

Fast-forward to 2012, where another October Surprise stole the attention of the nation's media. Hurricane Sandy and the appropriate response by the Obama Administration gave the president weighty press attention in his emergency management role as "Consoler-in-Chief". Acknowledgment by Republican Governor Chris Christie for the federal government's quick and effective reaction to the hurricane-battered New Jersey Coast provided significant fodder for media pundits. After heaping praise on Obama, Gov. Christie (a key supporter and surrogate of Republican presidential candidate Mitt Romney) was photographed embracing the President. Social media went viral and many undecided voters backed President Obama who appeared, in the aftermath of the hurricane, willing to cross party lines for the good of the country.

Each October Surprise had its own unique impact on the presidential election that occurred in the month or months after coming to light. Many smaller national races and local/state campaigns have experienced their own surprises in the walk-up to Election Day. Look no further than the 2017 allegations of child molestation and sexual harassment that withered Alabama U.S. Senate candidate Roy Moore in the weeks before his epic loss to Doug Jones. However, the most extensive October Surprise (really a combination of shocking and damaging political revelations) hit the 2016 campaign in early October. The repercussions of the day would stick to Trump like concrete through the election and beyond. The weight of the embarrassing and politically destructive revelations of the day would all but cement the 2016 race in the history books, forever re-writing the preconceived notion of a bombshell campaign interruption.

October 7th, 2016, was just a usual autumn day in a fiery presidential campaign...at least it was until mid-afternoon when the monotonous routine became anything but dull. A major storm cell from the Western Atlantic was on its way to cause devastation in Florida and along the southern American seaboard having left Haiti, Cuba, and the Bahamas in shambles. Hurricane Matthew was consuming much of the media coverage, a saddening respite from the tumultuous presidential political operation that had dominated the news for over a year. President Obama and both campaigns were briefed on the looming Category 4 storm off the coast of Florida – an electoral goldmine focused on by both Trump and Clinton in the final months. Yet the ferocious meteorological depression that ultimately took the lives of forty-seven Americans was not to be the headline of the day. It quickly became lost in the bizarre press coverage that developed hours later.

As far back as early summer of 2016, American intelligence agencies intercepted chatter of potential Russian involvement in the U.S. elections. The extent to the foreign intrusion was unknown, but the Russian Federation had previously interrupted elections in several former Soviet satellite states. Bits and pieces came together slowly. By the fall however, American intelligence networks had begun to construct an assessment of Russia's interjection on the U.S. 2016 presidential contest.

There's a famous quote by Maya Angelou, one that continuously came up during the 2016 presidential contest that contends, "When someone shows you who they are, believe them." It perfectly described the argument of the Clinton campaign (even several GOP primary challengers) regarding the vulgarity and indecency of Donald Trump during the election cycle. The line should have included the much-needed provision...don't let them walk it back for political gain. After all, that was the Trump camp's strategy...to strike down their candidate's previous comments, inappropriate off-prompter arguments, and outright insulting lies.

For months, the Trump Campaign had been outlining the narrative that the election would be unfair with the candidate perpetuating claims that the election would be "rigged". His allegation was that election manipulation would be to Clinton's benefit, not his, even though he provided no proof of such manipulation. As a result of the narrative the Trump camp had been peddling, the Obama Administration and U.S. Intelligence organizations were worried about sharing information on foreign tampering with the electoral process. James Clapper (Director of National Intelligence), Jeh Johnson (Secretary of Department of Homeland Security), and the White House were nervous about creating chaos by exposing their confidence of Russian involvement. They equally were concerned of public perceptions or campaign push back if they retained the information.

If it were leaked or made public after the election that the U.S. government had been aware of Russian attempts to tip the scale towards one candidate, anarchy might ensue. The risk of pandemonium would exponentially grow if the Intelligence Community and Obama Administration appeared to have knowingly allowed Russia to interfere without alerting the public. Administration officials ultimately agreed that the voters and both campaigns deserved to know about Russia's ongoing attempts to push the campaign in a controlled direction. They chose transparency

– opting to stop withholding from the American people their continuing investigation into foreign involvement.

The Obama Administration and the U.S. Intelligence Community contemporaneously chose October 7th as the day to bring to light information about a foreign government's interaction in the U.S. elections process. Administration officials felt the need to make public the information that American intelligence sources had uncovered – recognizing the failure to illuminate the electorate to outside influence would cast a shadow of doubt on the fair and unadulterated electoral process the country deserved. Little did they know, the shocking assertions they prepared to disseminate would barely even make the chyrons or crawling news ticker banners of media outlets by the end of the day.

Around 3:00 PM Eastern, the Administration released a statement accusing Russian intelligence organizations of meddling in the presidential elections. Intel had been gathered over months, leading the Director of National Intelligence (DNI) and the greater American Intelligence Community to surmise that the Russian government was behind pointed email and database hacks. According to their understanding at the time, the foreign cyber intrusion was limited to Democratic National Committee and Clinton Campaign aligned servers. DNI Clapper and Secretary Johnson released a joint public statement, suggesting the Kremlin had utilized stolen emails to disturb the American presidential election process. The statement detailed:

"The U.S. Intelligence Community (USIC) is confident that the Russian Government directed the recent compromises of e-mails from US persons and institutions, including from US political organizations. The recent disclosures of alleged hacked e-mails on sites like DCLeaks.com and WikiLeaks and by the Guccifer 2.0 online persona are consistent

with the methods and motivations of Russian-directed efforts. These thefts and disclosures are intended to interfere with the US election process... Secretary Johnson and DHS officials are working directly with the National Association of Secretaries of State to offer assistance, share information, and provide additional resources to state and local officials."

– Joint Statement from the DHS and the office of the DNI on Election Security (October 7, 2016)

The breaking news of the day had only just begun to roll in; by comparison, the Administration's release of intelligence findings was chump change to what was about to come. Also brewing that morning, unbeknownst to the Obama Administration, the *Washington Post* was working to corroborate a story that had the potential to blow up the campaign and change the course of history. David Fahrenthold, an investigative journalist at *The Post*, had received a scintillating story around 11:00 AM Eastern complete with a provocative video and an audio recording of incredible significance. Reporters on Fahrenthold's team and the *Washington Post*'s legal consultants had been at work putting together a story that was sure to become front-page news in every media market across America. The *Washington Post* editorial staff knew they were on a short timescale – the race was on to release the story before another paper or one of the networks got wind of the incendiary video clip. If they beat their competition, the story they had to share would surely cause an uproar at water coolers nationwide, perhaps even detonating the already contentious powder keg fueling the nation's hostile political debate. They knew within minutes after its release, the video would be played, analyzed, and discussed on every network, quickly becoming a trending topic on every social media platform. At 4:02 PM Eastern, the *Washington Post* story broke.

Trump: *"I moved on her, actually. You know, she was down on Palm Beach. I moved on her, and I failed. I'll admit it...I did try and fuck her. She was married. I moved on her very heavily. In fact, I took her out furniture shopping. She wanted to get some furniture. I said, "I'll show you where they have some nice furniture." I took her out furniture — I moved on her like a bitch. But I couldn't get there. And she was married. Then all of a sudden I see her, she's now got the big phony tits and everything. She's totally changed her look."*

Billy Bush: *"Sheesh, your girl's hot as shit. In the purple."*
Trump: *"Whoa! Whoa!"*
Bush: *"Yes! The Donald has scored. Whoa, my man!"*
Trump: *"Yeah, that's her. With the gold. I better use some Tic Tacs just in case I start kissing her. You know, I'm automatically attracted to beautiful — I just start kissing them. It's like a magnet. Just kiss. I don't even wait. And when you're a star, they let you do it. You can do anything."*
Bush: *"Whatever you want."*
Trump: *"Grab 'em by the pussy. You can do anything."*
Bush: *"Uh, yeah, those legs, all I can see is the legs."*
Trump: *"Oh, it looks good."*

–Excerpts from the *Access Hollywood* Tape originally reported by David Fahrenthold at the *Washington Post*. (October 7, 2016)

A 5 minute 22 second video obtained by *The Washington Post* featured a 2005 dialogue between *Access Hollywood* correspondent Billy Bush and then businessman Donald Trump. The two were on a bus en-route to a taping of the popular daytime soap *Days of our Lives* where Trump was set to appear. While navigating the NBC Studios in Burbank, California, Trump acknowledged to

Bush, unaware he was being recorded, "when you're a star, you can do anything" including groping and assaulting women. The video clip didn't show the conversation, as there was minimal video showing the inside of the bus, but the audio was clearly matched to the television personality and businessman. Video of Trump and Bush exiting the motor coach to meet with an actress on the soap opera confirmed the conversation was between the two men whose recognizable voices matched perfectly with the audiotape.

The *Washington Post* sent requests for comment to both Billy Bush and the Trump Campaign in the hours before going live with the story on the newspaper's website. According to Fahrenthold, Billy Bush and his PR team refused to comment while the Trump campaign deliberated their official response to the story. Originally only presented a copy of the video's transcript, the Trump campaign pushed back arguing that the tenor of the remarks was unlike Mr. Trump. In the final minutes before publishing the story and only after receiving a copy of the video of the tour bus interview, the Trump campaign confirmed via statement to the *Washington Post* that Mr. Trump was responsible for the remarks. In their retort, the campaign shrugged off the tape as a private conversation, believed to be off-the-record, and nothing more than an example of boys being boys. Trump's team doubled down, suggesting that Bill Clinton was guilty of far worse behavior. Unlike the former president, Trump had only talked about such behavior implying allegations against the 42nd President were naughtier than what was on the tape.

At 4:02 PM Eastern, the *Washington Post* published their story complete with the Trump campaign response and the 5-minute video clip. Just minutes later, NBC released their own version of the story followed quickly by comments from nearly every major media outlet. Within the hour, the story was plastered on Facebook and Twitter posts, scrolling across the bottom of news screens, and shared with millions around the globe. All eyes were glued to the TV, and ears perked up, watching and listening to the graphic audio of the tape and the nearly seamless coverage and debate on cable news channels. The video shocked everyone – many believing (in that moment) the clip represented the final straw of the Trump campaign, a turning point in the race, and the end of Donald Trump's involvement in presidential politics.

The Clinton campaign senior staff were reportedly still meeting about the earlier developments of Russian involvement disseminated by the U.S. Intelligence Community when news of the scandalous video broke. They had been crafting a message to share the intelligence report, information that appeared to suggest Russia was working to damage Clinton and benefit Trump. Like most of the country, the Clinton camp was caught completely off guard by the *Access Hollywood* tape. It has been widely reported they felt the October Surprise would define the final weeks of the campaign. Meanwhile many amongst the Trump campaign felt the tape was an attack from the left, perhaps even opposition research from the Clinton team designed to damage the businessman before the second presidential debate, just two days away, in St. Louis Missouri. But wait, there was more...

At roughly 4:32 PM Eastern, a mere thirty minutes after what appeared to be the most destructive campaign blow in American political history, a second story came to light. Whistleblower nonprofit Wikileaks dumped thousands of pages of emails stolen from the Clinton Campaign Chairman John Podesta's private email account. Some of the message chains dumped by this scandalmonger Internet transparency (and possibly hacking) organization included partial transcripts of Secretary Clinton's paid speeches to investment groups and Wall Street banks. The propagation of the email cache was designed to damage the Clinton campaign, but its timing may have indicated a more sinister and dubious motive too.

Jennifer Palmieri (the Clinton Campaign Director of Communications) has suggested the release of the Podesta emails – on the same day as the Russian meddling statement and *Access Hollywood* tape – was possibly a distraction meant to cover up the two bigger stories of the day. While little has been discussed about Wikileaks' intentions or decision to release the trove of hijacked emails on October 7th, 2016, Palmieri maintains that the email dump was "obviously not an accident". The question surrounding Wikileaks' motivation in dropping the emails on that particular Friday afternoon, just 30 minutes after the *Access Hollywood* story broke, remains one of the biggest unanswered questions of the 2016 campaign cycle.

Culminating one of the most incredible days in American politics, the Trump campaign issued a filmed statement that addressed the damaging *Access Hollywood* tape. Set against a blue cityscape backdrop, Donald Trump himself delivered an explanation of the video and made comments on the 2005 conversation. Trump insisted his words were merely "locker room talk" and didn't match the severity of what others had said or done. He acknowledged that he was not a "perfect person nor pretended to be someone he was not". He apologized and quickly pivoted his video statement to accuse Bill Clinton of "abusing women" and Hillary of shaming, bullying, and intimidating the victims of Bill's alleged assaults.

Perhaps most disgusting to many who tuned in to late night television and cable news coverage of the locker room talk discussion was the Trump response. Not only did the presidential candidate try to write off the despicable rhetoric as something that other men also normally engaged in, but he proclaimed that he really had great respect for women. The man, seen coming off the bus and the corresponding voice that shared his real feelings about the fairer sex, tried to convince voters he cared about women and respected them. To most appalled viewers, the video and paralleling audio indicated otherwise.

By the following morning, the hurricane thrashing Florida and the revelation of Russian involvement in the electoral process were nearly absent from the press. The Wikileaks email unload and *Access Hollywood* interview consumed the attention of the country and headlined every major newspaper. Below the fold, in text far smaller than the byline attributing the raunchy video story to the *Washington Post*'s Fahrenthold, one might have found mention of the Intelligence Community's statement, but it's unlikely many read those less scintillating articles. The country would have to wait to discuss in detail the Russian Federation's Influence Campaign and the potential it had on the final race outcome.

For the next few days, the Internet and cable news was flooded with calls for Trump to drop out of the race leaving room for a Republican with less baggage to have a fighting chance against Clinton on November 8th. (Few believed Trump could overcome the scandal and win on Election Day without cheating or somehow trying to steal the election.) Prominent political figures including former Secretary of State Condoleezza Rice and Former Republican presidential candidate Mitt Romney both condemned the behavior expressed by Trump in the bus video. Rice suggested the candidate pull out of the 2016 race sharing on Facebook, "Enough! Donald Trump should not be President. He should withdraw." Romney tweeted his retort, "Hitting on married women? Condoning assault? Such vile degradations demean our wives and daughters and corrupt America's face to the world." It was the sitting Congressional politicians that threw the strongest punches. Utah Congressman Jason Chaffetz argued that he couldn't defend his support of Trump anymore, especially to his 15-year old daughter. Senator Jeff Flake of Arizona tweeted his disgust contending, "America deserved better than Donald Trump". Even the once presumed GOP nominee, Jeb Bush called out Trump's *Access Hollywood* comments adding, "as the grandfather of two precious girls, I find that no apology can excuse away Donald Trump's reprehensible comments degrading women." (Billy Bush, the *Access Hollywood* host who was recorded egging Trump on in the salacious tape, is the first cousin of Governor Jeb Bush and of former President George W. Bush. He lost his job after the release of the video.)

Politicians on the right, who just days before had been on the campaign trail stumping for Trump, began distancing themselves from the damaged Republican nominee. Over the course of a few hours, Trump's political capital was all but spent and predictions and rumors of a humiliating exit were growing in the media. Trump's 2005 comments on the *Access Hollywood* bus weren't just damaging to his White House aspirations, they also had potential catastrophic effects in down-ballot races. The blowout left Trump's team with a decision to make, either press on or bow out. The conservative hope to flip control of the government was on the line and it would be up to Trump to decide what would happen next.

According to Steve Bannon, the Chief Executive of the Trump Campaign, meetings regarding the future of the campaign were held the evening of the video's release. Consultations extended into the early morning hours. It has been extensively recounted that RNC Chairman Reince Priebus gave Trump two choices, "You either drop out right now, or you lose by the biggest landslide in American political history." Bannon had another idea. He asserted, "They don't care" and noted the broad coalition of supporters calling for the candidate to remain in the race. Ultimately, Trump sided with Bannon and the campaign quickly pivoted to redirect press questions about the tape to Bill Clinton's alleged infidelities. At rallies and events on the trail, Trump and the RNC maintained the cover of "Locker Room Talk" and continued to aggressively target the Clintons, drawing attention away from the *Access Hollywood* tape.

Although their testimony to the press didn't increase the political consequence for Trump, his friends from adolescence corroborated the nature of their former peer. Donald's classmates at NYMA suggested that the young playboy learned about women from the magazine of the same name (*Playboy*) and the behavior in the video was not outside of the businessman's norm. They cited recollections of inappropriate discussions he and his roommates had in the barracks of the military academy and how that manner of discussing women stayed with Trump after graduation. The "barracks talk" Trump engaged in during his youth transformed to "locker room talk" in the businessman's adult life. The principle of the discussion was the same, the vocabulary was the same...just the name used to shield the degrading conversations had been altered.

CHAPTER SEVEN: COMEY AND THE INVESTIGATION THAT NEVER WAS

Although it never became a serious criminal investigation, Clinton was plagued by the email scandal brought to light before she announced her candidacy and amplified in the Democratic primaries. Worry that a potential President Clinton could be subpoenaed to testify in front of Congress or a special council made many liberal voters uneasy. Supporters of her Democratic rival, Senator Bernie Sanders, were especially concerned, most having only barely warmed to the idea of a Clinton president after a long primary battle.

Back in 2001 as a U.S. Senator, Hillary operated in the usual way, taking calls and sending emails via her Blackberry smartphone – a device commonly used by government employees at the time. Her email was hosted through Blackberry's Enterprise Server, which at the time was the most secure mobile communications system (hence the frequent use of the devices among other Washington political elites). Then-Senator Barack Obama was also known to enjoy the use of Blackberry products, keeping his device clipped to his belt until as president the Secret Service took it away for security concerns. Clinton's device, however, was never seized when she became the Secretary of State in early January of 2009. Instead, her staff at the State Department looked for a solution to Clinton's desire to continue using a single smartphone for email exchange, rather than the suggested secure workstation that could be installed in her office in Foggy Bottom.

As early as spring of 2007, Senator Clinton set-up an email server in her Chappaqua, New York home ahead of her first presidential campaign in 2008. The system was later used as the primary server for Hillary's emails during her tenure at the State Department. Many at the Department and within the American Intelligence Community knew that Clinton's email was run through a non-traditional process for a government office holder of her rank. Instead of using the normal .gov domain, Clinton's emails originated from clintonemail.com, registered along with 13 other domains to the Clintons. The email addresses, including hdr22@clintonemail.com and hrod17@clintonemail.com, used by Hillary for official business were not encrypted to government security standards, although every email sent or received by government systems transferring through the Chappaqua server was encoded.

Government employees and a handful of outsiders had knowledge of the private email server used by Secretary Clinton long before she left the State Department and declared her candidacy to succeed President Obama. Every government staffer at the State Department and the White House who corresponded with Clinton via email (including President Obama) knew their messages were not going to a .gov address. It's unclear how many recognized that her correspondence wasn't being captured by the government system designed to archive all administration emails for preservation. Furthermore, it remains unclear how many senior administration staffers were aware that the server hosting Clinton's email was located in her home and not equipped with an encryption level befitting an employee with a Yankee White security clearance (Top Secret/Crypto/SCI). Nevertheless, it was considered acceptable to those who knew Clinton wasn't using a government email. Under the absence of law, she was allowed to do so, provided her emails to Obama Administration staff were snapshot for preservation on one end. All of the email exchanges between Clinton and government employees with .gov email addresses would automatically be recorded by the government system for appropriate screening and archival.

Previous Secretaries of State also maintained personal email accounts similar to Hillary. However, it wasn't just the nation's top diplomats that opted out of using a .gov email account as their primary method of official correspondence. Numerous conservative politicians also maintained private email servers while holding high offices, including 2016 GOP primary candidates former Florida Gov. Jeb Bush, Wisconsin Gov. Scott Walker, Florida Sen. Marco Rubio, New Jersey Gov. Chris Christie, former Texas Gov. Rick Perry, and Louisiana Gov. Bobby Jindal.

Even the Bush Administration had its own history of employing private email accounts during public service. One of Clinton's predecessors, Former Secretary Colin Powell (R), used a private email address during his tenure, although his wasn't hosted on a server in his home. As part of a Congressional investigation at the end of the Bush Administration in 2007, it was disclosed that White House senior staff used email and pagers provided by the Republican National Committee. The RNC apparently supplied email access to Bush 43 personnel via a hosted server in their offices within the District allowing staff to communicate without conversations becoming unmasked under Congressional investigation or public disclosure. Senior Advisor Karl Rove, White House Chief of Staff Andrew Card, White House Director of Political Affairs Ken Mehlman, and staff in the Communications Office used the RNC's arrangement to circumvent the government automatic-archive system and provisions of the Hatch Act. At least 88 accounts were furnished by the RNC for use by the White House, many staffers using them as their primary or only email address. Even Sarah Palin, the female starlet of the Republican Party, and former GOP nominee Mitt Romney used private email during their time in elected office.

Widespread public knowledge of Hillary using a private email account came to light by early 2013 after a Romanian hacker operating under the portmanteau pseudonym Guccifer (Gucci Lucifer) dumped a trove of emails between Clinton and her former adviser Sidney Blumenthal. Within months, connections were being made between the emails released by Guccifer and the likelihood that Clinton had maintained a private email server during her tenure as head of the State Department. In light of continued Congressional investigations into the attacks in Benghazi, questions regarding Clinton's communications with diplomatic staff and her personal aids came to light. FOIA (Freedom of Information Act) requests were sent to the State Department seeking detailed email threads between the Secretary and State staff involved in these investigations.

In 2014, as the United States House Select Committee on Benghazi, led by Republican Congressional Representatives, ramped up its investigation of the State Department and Secretary Clinton, the email drama was brought into focus. This time the State Department was center stage with senior staff realizing they didn't have the copies of email exchanges between Clinton and senior advisors that the committee was requesting. As a result, the State Department dispatched letters to former Secretaries of State (those who served during the age of email) asking them to provide any documents they had from their respective tenure at the Department. Along with information from Secretaries Albright, Powell, and Rice, Clinton provided a dozen boxes of transcripts containing over 30,000 pages of email exchanges.

While the State Department was initially sufficiently pleased with the hand over of Clinton Era emails, it was quickly made known that the Secretary had retained over 32,000 emails. She had chosen to hand over only the exchanges she and her legal team deemed were related to matters of State. The 32,000 emails Clinton held onto were deemed of a "personal" nature and not part of her business as a representative of the U.S. government. Clinton would later identify them as relating to family vacations, the planning of her daughter Chelsea's wedding, and the former First Lady's weekly yoga routine.

When there's smoke, there's not always fire – sometimes it's just a dumpster smoldering across the street. So was the case in the Clinton email scandal – just another trumped up (pun intended) right-wing attack against a Democratic American leader. Had the roles been reversed, liberals would have undoubtedly raised questions about the emails, but conservative media would have walked back any arguments that a GOP politician was trying to subterfuge the American electorate or break the law. (Did those Republican candidates "not recall" they had used similar private email accounts, or did they not see the hypocrisy of their argument against Clinton?)

The argument used by the Bush Administration would have made for a better line of reasoning than what the Clinton camp generated. The RNC email server gave coverage to White House staff to engage in politics without violating the Hatch Act. Instead, the Clinton camp maintained that the Secretary was simply using the personal server and corresponding private email because of the convenience it provided in limiting the number of devices she needed. Rather than requiring a secure communications device to correspond with officials in Foggy Bottom, the Situation Room, or even the President in the Oval, Clinton could use the same device she used to stay in touch with her husband and daughter...especially as she was helping plan Chelsea's wedding.

Clinton was often pictured reading emails on her Blackberry device during her four-year term as Secretary of State. Many Internet memes (a social media phenomena) postulated what the Secretary might be texting or who she was communicating with. Although the country was having fun guessing who was in Clinton's contacts folder, few knew where the emails she received on her Blackberry were hosted. When the news finally came to light, it caught many off guard. Even the most ardent Clinton supporters recognize that Clinton should have known better than to use a personal server. The Secretary could have easily avoided the PR nightmare email scandal by using a government server on a secure device in her office. After struggling through the Lewinsky Scandal, an offshoot of the Whitewater Investigation during Bill's presidency, establishment Democrats were upset to see another controversy come to light surrounding their party's favorite to win in 2016. Like the previous public embarrassments the Clintons had undergone, the email controversy was politically charged and was predicated on a Congressional investigation meant to damage the iconic American political family's public image.

As a result of eight Congressional committees investigating the September 11, 2012 attack on American diplomats in Benghazi, Libya, the email controversy gained national attention in conservative media. By the time the House Select Committee on Benghazi (the 8th Congressional investigation) started holding hearings, the email scandal was being blown-up on Fox News, traditional conservative print media, and right-wing Internet sites. The emails and Clinton's private email server quickly became a central part of the Benghazi Investigation led by GOP Representative Trey "the Bulldog" Gowdy (R) of South Carolina's 4th District. That investigation, like the previous seven, would trickle into the hemisphere of political bias, choosing to focus almost solely on Clinton's role in the State Department's actions before, during, and after the attacks.

A core part of the Clinton email investigation brought to light by FBI Director James Comey stemmed from the Benghazi investigations. Republican Congressmen publicly harangued Clinton during hearings causing biased reports to be generated by majority committee members. Those files, quickly leaked to the press, made Clinton appear responsible for the deaths of four Americans including U.S. Ambassador to Libya J. Christopher Stevens. Coming to a climax during the fall of 2015, the House Select Committee on Benghazi accepted Clinton's request to publicly answer questions of the Committee – a hope of Hillary and her campaign looking to damper the false stories of her responsibility in the 9/11/2012 attack.

On October 22nd, 2015, Clinton appeared before the House Select Committee, delivering a brief statement before answering questions for almost 11 hours. It made for absolutely appalling television watching conservative Congressional Representatives disrespect, denigrate, and launch downright ridiculous accusations at Hillary Clinton for 11 HOURS! The questioning was clearly biased on both sides though. Democrats asked questions that allowed Clinton to make larger statements and direct the narrative, while Republican Representatives directly targeted the former Secretary. One even asked if Clinton was at home "alone" on the night of the attack in Libya, playfully insinuating that the Secretary may have been having an affair. Congresswoman Martha Roby of Alabama was pressing Clinton on her access to secure communications (a precursor to a launch into questions pertaining to Clinton's email server) when she asked if Clinton had the capability to receive sensitive compartmentalized communications at her home. Clinton said she did. In response, Roby asked if Clinton was home alone. "I was alone, yes." Clinton said. Roby continued, "The whole night?" "Well yes, the whole night." Clinton replied erupting into her well-known vociferous laughter. "I don't know why that's funny. Did you have any in-person briefings? I don't find it funny at all," the Alabama Representative rebuked. "A little note of levity at 7:15 PM." Clinton answered. "Congresswoman," Clinton continued, "I had secure phones, I had other equipment that kept me in touch with the State Department at all times. I did not sleep all night. I was very much focused on what we were doing."

The moment was widely shared by both sides, complete with vastly different accompanying narratives. The right arguing that Clinton was laughing off the deaths of four American diplomats, the left maintaining that Clinton humorously responded to a ridiculous politically-influenced question. As the investigation came to an end in the weeks following Clinton's testimony, it was made extraordinarily clear that the central directive of the House Select Committee on Benghazi was to subvert Clinton's presidential ambitions by damaging her image and impugning her credibility as a diplomat. House Majority Leader Kevin McCarthy (R-CA) provided the explanation for the GOP interrogatory of Secretary Clinton. He shared on *The Sean Hannity Show*, "Everybody thought Hillary Clinton was unbeatable, right? But we put together a Benghazi special committee, a select committee. What are her numbers today? Her numbers are dropping. Why? Because she's untrustable [sic]. But no one would have known any of that had happened, had we not fought." The obsequious attacks by Republican Congressional Representatives against the distinguished former Secretary of State, as part of a larger conservative agenda focused on derailing the Hillary for America campaign, failed.

The battle wounds of the Benghazi Investigation nevertheless festered in the continuous coverage of Clinton's email controversy by right-wing media outlets. The investigations couldn't bring Clinton down, but damage was rendered through the persistent criticism her email scandal generated. The emails would remain a core conservative talking point through the summer of 2016, notably coming back into the spotlight in the final month of the campaign as part of Clinton's own October Surprise.

So, while Trump was dealing with his share of problems on October 7th, 2016, Clinton's campaign was presented with a new challenge when Campaign Chair John Podesta's emails were leaked by Wikileaks. The introduction of these emails, this time belonging to a Clinton campaign advisor and close confidant, only ramped up the attacks from the right. For weeks prior, the campaign had been making positive strides in agreeing to consider releasing Hillary's personal emails demanded by the right if the Trump campaign published their candidate's tax returns. Amongst these new emails were partial transcripts of Hillary's speeches to Wall Street firms and banks. These excerpts (edited out of context by Wikileaks) didn't help with the campaign's attempts to back away from the opposition's narrative. It made Clinton appear to be in the pocket of Wall Street and supported by the big banks instead of by middle-class America.

While the Billy Bush interview of her opponent was consuming much of the press, the Clinton campaign was feverishly walking back this newly dumped trove of stolen emails. Between the two stories, there was little room for the Russian intervention allegations made by the Intelligence Community. All of the major media outlets were airing round-the-clock coverage of the bus video and updates from Podesta's emails, but a bigger revelation with even greater significance to the election was looming. Though millions of mail-in, early voting, and absentee ballots had already been collected, a shocking newsbreak, with the potential to throw the race, was about to come to light. What is today referred to as the biggest story of the 2016 campaign dropped like a bombshell only ten days before the election. An explosive shock it was...albeit a botched one that did more damage than good.

On October 28th, just 11 days before the election, Federal Bureau of Investigation Director James "Jim" Comey dropped a political atomic warhead by sending Congress a letter informing them that the FBI was reopening its investigation of Clinton's emails. New evidence obtained as part of an unrelated investigation of Anthony Weiner (the estranged husband of Clinton's aide Huma Abedin) suggested more unseen emails were available to be checked for the presence of classified material. In the days that followed, it became clear that the emails found on a joint Abedin-Weiner laptop were merely duplicates of correspondence already examined. A second letter was consequently sent to Congress just two days before the election where Comey acknowledged that no new evidence was found and the investigation was to remain closed, but it was too late. The damage was done!

The investigation by the FBI into Clinton's emails had begun as soon as the Justice Department was made aware that classified emails or correspondence, which included restricted material, might have been transmitted through the private server in Clinton's New York home. FBI Director Comey identified over a hundred emails that contained information that had been marked as classified at the time they were sent. Over two thousand email chains from Clinton's server were retroactively marked as classified by the State Department. Several emails were labeled with a (C) marking, denoting they were confidential in nature, though Clinton argued she was uninformed of the meaning of the (C) notation. In concert with the State Department, the FBI investigated the emails provided by Clinton's legal team, ultimately acknowledging on July 5th, 2016, that the FBI's investigation had concluded. Director Comey deemed Clinton was "extremely careless" in her handling of confidential and classified digital materials but argued that her actions weren't criminal. He recommended that the U.S. Attorney General (Loretta Lynch) not press charges against the Secretary. The generally unbiased *New York Times* made the case that if Clinton received classified emails, she might not have known that they contained secure information or classified materials. They contend that the "occasional appearance of classified information" in the Clinton account was probably of "marginal consequence".

It's understandable why Clinton wanted to retain control of her emails. After decades of being held to a different standard than her male counterparts, Clinton was (and still is) cautious, analyzing each step before she makes it. Retaining control of her communication, both work-related and private, gave her the ability to control what did and didn't leak. The email scandal from the beginning was more politically motivated than aimed at addressing a blunder by the former Secretary of State. The constant drip, drip, drip of attacks against Clinton, from Benghazi to the use of a private email server, even after the investigation into the controversy was closed, demonstrated the concern that led her to preserve her record of electronic correspondence internally in the first place.

Conservatives kept the story on the emails, arguing that Clinton had wiped her server to hide evidence of inappropriate communications or illegal activities she may have been involved in. Clinton's jovial rebuke of those allegations (replying to questions from the press if she had wiped the server by saying with jest, "what, with a cloth?") didn't buy her any support. Republicans also suggested that a happenstance meeting between Attorney General Lynch and Bill Clinton on the airport tarmac at Phoenix-Sky Harbor International was a concerted effort by the Clintons to force Lynch to downplay the email investigation. As both the Attorney General and Clintons maintain, the meeting was by coincidence, "primarily social", and did not include any discussion by the two of pending investigations.

Did Secretary Clinton make a mistake? Yes. Did she take

responsibility and corrective action? Yes. Did she deserve to be investigated? Yes! Did she deserve that investigation to become a political tool aimed at derailing her presidential ambitions? NO! Yet that is exactly what happened. The political right pounced on the emails and flooded the news with the scandal. Clinton's misguided and improper use of a personal email was not illegal under the law, but in the court of public opinion, the Secretary was guilty...of something.

In the months following the public disclosure of Clinton's email scandal, it was made clear that the Secretary had a SCIF in her DC home, in addition to secure communications equipment at her office in Foggy Bottom and the capabilities available at the White House. The Sensitive Compartmented Information Facility (SCIF), basically a secure room with encrypted communications systems, would have allowed Clinton to conduct business without needing a personal email. In hindsight, the Secretary only put herself at risk by using a private email. That realization would become clear during the 2016 campaign, on Election Night, and in her memoir *What Happened*, published in late summer of 2017.

The email scandal that had been looming over the Clinton campaign was reason for worry to many voters. Questions had arisen about legal hurdles the scandal could cause a potential Clinton presidency should an indictment or subpoena of a President Hillary Clinton occur. Legal analysts had deliberated for months on every major network arguing over the liability, responsibility, negligence, and technological naivety of the Democrat in her use of a personal email server while employed as the U.S. Secretary of State. Doubts had circled the candidate's claim that she had handed over all "work-related emails" to the State Department.

The issue was quickly a partisan production with right-wing media exacerbating rumors and making outlandish suggestions of possible corruption by Secretary Clinton, her campaign, or her legal team. Clinton had been out of the State Department since January of 2013, but her emails had remained in the spotlight. Her political enemies quickly jumped at the scandal, making early blows in an attempt to derail her presumed 2016 presidential run before it started. Clinton pressed on through the November 2016 elections with the scandal looming overhead every step of the way.

CHAPTER EIGHT: ELECTION NIGHT

It was to be the turning point of a centuries old power struggle between men and women – a landmark event that would change the way politics in America functioned forever. Election Night 2016 would be like every other before it, only this time America was going to elect the first woman president of the United States, the first female leader of the free world. An international audience would watch as results came in state by state, guaranteeing a historic win for Hillary Clinton, the Democratic Party, and women around the globe who were watching in earnest, waiting for the groundbreaking moment to happen. Then it didn't...

Tuesday, November 8th began with the crest of a beautiful sunrise on the East Coast, excellent weather across the fifty states other than a few pockets of the country experiencing some light rain. (Weather is important on election days as voters stay home if it's raining or too cold outside.) Other than scattered showers in Illinois and Texas, this Tuesday was perfect – a great day for a historic election. The significance of the day wasn't lost on voters as they dutifully headed to the ballot box. America was ready for a bright capstone to a dark and divisive election that had been tearing the country apart for over a year. Finally, the grueling process was hours from its climax – the coronation of the 45th President of the United States – the transition of power from one administration to the next. Both campaigns descended on New York City for their respective Election Night watch parties; one would have a blast after the results came in but there'd be no fireworks for the losing team.

The Trump campaign packed the New York Hilton-Midtown with GOP elites, high-rolling contributors, and campaign insiders. They nervously awaited what had been looming for months, a decisive end to the campaign the businessman had started 17 months earlier on an escalator in Trump Tower. Just like he had on that first day of the campaign, Trump would descend from his penthouse apartment to address a crowd of loyal supporters, only this time he'd be delivering a concession speech. The campaign that had been as damaging to America's image as it was to Donald Trump's brand was near its finale, only 136 million votes to be tallied. The candidate himself had voted earlier in the day at a Manhattan public school. The cameras even caught Donald peeking at his wife's ballot to make sure she voted for the right candidate. Did she? Both Trumps joined millions of Americans in casting their vote to determine the future of the country.

Secretary Clinton and former President Bill Clinton went to the polls early, voting near their home in Chappaqua, New York before heading into the city to watch the election results in the Democratic candidate's war room. Party leaders, fellow politicians, and future nominees would stand alongside the candidate's staff and supporters as they were about to watch history unfold.

Make America Stronger Together Again

The Hillary for America campaign would play host to a massive Election Night Gala at the Jacob K. Javits Convention Center on New York City's waterfront, overlooking the Hudson River. This colossal convention space, once promoted by Clinton's opponent, was certain to be the site of a historic victory speech if everything went according to plan. Everyone in attendance planned on watching the Secretary become the president-elect. When the final electoral math was computed and under a literal glass ceiling, Hillary Clinton would make history and inspire millions around the globe. Rockets would illuminate the darkness that had encompassed the 2016 campaign cycle.

The U.S. Secret Service was in overdrive on November 8th, covering the security needs of the two principle protectees, their running mates, and families. Under the glimmering lights of Manhattan's cityscape, a monumental night was in store for the Big Apple. The Javits Center and the Hilton-Midtown, only a mile and a half apart, were the two safest sites in America, yet one would never guess as the feelings of excitement, hopefulness, and nervousness had everyone in the city on edge. High hopes were abounding in New York and across the country as millions tuned in to see if their candidate of choice would have a good night once polls closed. The air was thick with anticipation, everyone watching and waiting for the final results, joyful that the end of an ugly campaign was finally in sight.

Television media was abuzz bringing in live commentary and animated interviews with voters who'd cast their ballots. Exit polling data from unofficial sources showed a decent turnout, not the biggest, but not small enough to cause concern either. Discussions over the electoral math, as well as predictions of battleground state winners, kept the pulse of the fast-paced finish to a long drawn-out competition. The race that had divided families but had also brought communities together was about to conclude. The clock ticked slowly as 8:00 Eastern neared, the start of Election Night and the end of the 2016 electoral process.

Results came in quickly at first, although only three states could be called at 8 o'clock – Vermont for Clinton, Kentucky and Indiana for Trump. No surprises. More and more states started to change color, shifting from the neutral gray to conservative red or liberal blue. Trump took the South and lower Midwest, while Clinton led in New England and on the West Coast. Again no surprises. Yet as the final polls closed across the country, concern started to shift direction. States expected to go easily for Clinton (based on pre-election polling data and exit polls at ballot boxes) started leaning more conservative than expected. The predictable solid blue states fell into the too-close-to-call category and then slipped slowly in Trump's favor.

Political analysts were in shock; what was happening? For months, Hillary Clinton had led the national public opinion polls, though the margin started to decrease in the final weeks. Going into Election Day, she was still favored to win handily, likely exceeding 320 electoral votes and easily besting Trump to get the 270-vote absolute majority necessary for victory. Nearly every major poll showed an advantage to Clinton, especially among reliable indexes and polling aggregation groups. *FiveThirtyEight*, *Real Clear Politics*, *Talking Points Memo*, and *Gallup* had successfully predicted previous wins. Each projected a Clinton victory over Trump with *FiveThirtyEight* forecasting a lopsided 71.4% to 28.6% win for the former Secretary of State. Both campaigns had internal polls showing a similar turnout. In all, no one expected even the possibility of a Trump victory and Clinton defeat.

As voting data continued to trickle in, Trump began to accumulate more states, beating Clinton in battlegrounds and former blue strongholds by small margins, yet enough to win without necessitating an automatic recount. As the night progressed, states that had at one time been Democratic Party bastions fell to a wave of Trumpism, causing the electoral math to tighten and Clinton's road to 270 to thin. States in the Clinton column started to unbelievably flip to Trump as final tallies came in. Donald's camp was gaining ground while Hillary's team was losing sight of a win, let alone the expected landslide. Absent of any reason to think differently and short of advanced warnings to focus harder on predictable blue strongholds, the Clinton camp watched in real time as their candidate's substantial lead dwindled to a nail-biter. They were unable to do anything but stare speechless at the election results in utter disbelief.

At 3:00 AM Eastern, November 9th, Donald Trump secured the magic number to win the election, surpassing 270 Electoral College votes. The surprise victory caught everyone off guard, leaving voters stunned and TV newscasters speechless. Hillary Clinton lost the Electoral College vote to Donald Trump in a historic upset, opposite nearly every projection. While Trump bested Clinton in the archaic electoral mechanism, Hillary had won the popular vote with a surplus of 2.9 million votes. (Clinton 65,853,516 – Trump 62,984,825) For the 5th time in American history, the Electoral College selected a president who lost the popular vote of the people.

The razor-thin electoral margin and several key polls remained close. Going into the early morning hours of November 9th, many Americans had gone to sleep, not watching the upset unfold. Most, including Republicans, thought it was Clinton's night only to find out what really happened the next morning. The rest of us were glued to our screens, iPhones, iPads, MacBooks, and TVs, watching nervously as states began to slip away taking with them our chances for a monumental victory. We watched helplessly as America's future shifted from steadiness to uncertainty, the bewildering sensation feeling more titanic than epic. An expected impossibility became possible – then all too real.

The "Blue Wall" that had given Democrats wins in 2008 and 2012 and had been a stronghold in every race since Bill Clinton's victory in 1992 had fallen. Clinton lost in Pennsylvania, Michigan, and Wisconsin, though all three "Rust Belt" states went to Trump with small margins, less than 1% of the total vote. The Rust Belt had been compromised, ultimately deflating the feeling of hope and making way for the incredible and completely unexpected loss. Had Clinton won the three states, she would have had a majority; had she secured Pennsylvania, Michigan, and Wisconsin, she would have been the president-elect. Who knew that when Hillary Clinton suggested America "practice politics as the art of making what appears to be impossible possible" that we would put her advice into practice and use it against her.

The Trump campaign had a fantastic night, considering the nearly absolute belief that Donald's prospects for the presidency were impossible after the tumultuous campaign, three poor debate performances, and constant news scandals. Somehow, by early morning November 9th, Trump became the President-Elect of the United States of America. The city of New York went silent, an eerie feeling churning in the pit of everyone's stomachs. The fireworks expected to close out a Clinton victory speech, like the candidate herself, never made an appearance. With his family by his side, the unexpected President-Elect took the stage; his comb over coiffed so perfectly, it couldn't possibly be a toupee. Trump gave an unrehearsed speech to his supporters claiming victory for his campaign and increasing the nervous tension around the country.

Hillary never made an appearance at the Javits Center. Instead, the campaign sent Chairman John Podesta to the stage built beneath the largest glass ceiling in New York City and shaped like the country Clinton was supposed to lead. Podesta explained that the candidate would address the evening's events the next morning, buying time for the Democrat's speechwriters to craft concession remarks. The Electoral College loss was a complete surprise, not just to the plethora of Clinton supporters in attendance at the Election Night party, but also to the campaign and its candidate. None on the Clinton team imagined losing a "blue state" to Trump, let alone three, nor did they expect to fall short in the key swing states of Florida and Ohio. No one on Team Clinton had anticipated losing to the New York patrician and alleged billionaire in the Electoral College while coming out ahead in the popular vote. Everyone at Hillary For America had expected an early victory celebration with fireworks ringing in the new Clinton Era...a continuation of the progress made under President Obama and a return to the prosperity of the first Clinton Administration.

The realization that America might change overnight left the country in a state of shock. Republicans were nervous, weighing the benefits of an electoral win with the concerns of many that Donald Trump was unprepared and uncontrollable. Democrats were scared, feeling America was beginning to plunge toward autarchy. The majority of the country had supported Clinton or a third party candidate and now they faced the chilling reality that the "other guy" had won. Would America still be the same? Would the United States follow in the footsteps of other countries that historically handed over the reins of power to a heavy-handed populist? Surely the strength of our democracy would be strong enough to block despotism from stomping out our egalitarian foundations, but our republic is fragile...maybe 2016 will be the beginning of the end.

PART TWO: MOVING FORWARD

CHAPTER NINE: THE MORNING AFTER

The United States of America stepped back 50 years in the fight for equality on Election Night 2016. The future occupant of the Oval Office, whom America decided on that fateful night, was not an ally of change, but a staunch opponent of modernity and the fight for individual rights. The man selected by the Electoral College would prefer America reflect the "good ole days" of Jim Crow, trickle-down-economics, and "don't ask don't tell." On that night and the days to follow, it was clear the people would need to hold their leader accountable and would need to fight hard for the values, freedoms, and liberties our country stands for.

I watched the election play out on TV and in the press. I lived the election campaigning and discussing the political issues with everyday Americans in the streets of Iowa, Nebraska, Washington, California, Oregon, and Hawaii. I spoke with Americans from nearly every state, offering my endorsement of Clinton and her Stronger Together vision for the country. I felt the election take its grip on those around me, changing their attitudes towards policies and forcing them to get involved in the political space for the first time. A little piece of me died on Election Night watching the ascension of a candidate I despised into the esteemed presidential club I so respected. A new fire grew deep within me to get up, press on, and continue the fight for the America I want to see.

Like so many across our country, I was immediately taken aback by the historic, unprecedented, and incredibly unexpected loss of a politician and role model I revered. With exceptions, the majority of my colleagues expected a Clinton victory, and many of us couldn't wrap our heads around a Trump Administration. Never expecting him to win, I too was completely caught off guard and crushed to the point of tears and anger. I was so sure that Hillary would defeat the GOP nominee. I never even contemplated what a Donald Trump presidency would be like, beyond thoughts of ridiculous policies and a rebranding of the White House with TRUMP in gilded palatial letters.

Like many who were a part of the Clinton campaign effort, I was dumbfounded by the success of a candidate few thought was qualified – let alone intelligent enough to hold America's highest office. For months, the Clinton camp had doubled down on Trump's inexperience, touting the line that he was "temperamentally unfit and grossly unqualified" for the presidency. They argued that in comparison to a former Secretary of State, two-term U.S. Senator, First Lady of the United States, Governor's spouse, lawyer, civil rights activist, philanthropist, and domestic policy advisor, Trump could never be expected to stand up to the Clinton machine.

For years we had jestingly thrown around the idea of a President Trump in good fun, but certainly not because we wanted to see it happen. Comedians had joked about what a Trump presidency would look like, but that was before the campaign...where the dark and vulgar side of Trump was paired with the malevolence of his tone and the demagoguery of his rhetoric. In the 2010's, '11s, and '12s, it was a joke that a conceited playboy with no political experience could be the president our country was waiting for – the conservative opposite of Barack Obama. Today it's still a joke; unfortunately it's one that's based in reality. Regrettably, there's no immediate happy ending to this comical presidency turned real-life nightmare.

On November 9th, Clinton officially conceded the election to Donald Trump, giving a speech to her closest supporters, campaign staff, and a massive contingent of reporters. Everyone in attendance and watching on TV was still dumbfounded by the late night electoral defeat. Dressed in purple, surrounded by her family and close aides, and holding back her emotions, Clinton called for her supporters to continue the fight and not lose hope in America. She advised the young women and girls watching to get back up when they get knocked down and "never believe that they can't or shouldn't go on."

Suspicions were raised almost immediately about the legitimacy of the Clinton defeat with millions of Americans calling on the losing candidates (Clinton, Green Party candidate Jill Stein, and Libertarian Gary Johnson) to challenge the election results. Appeals to terminate the Trump presidency before the country was forced to suffer through a four-year term sparked a new national discussion. Some called out the need to appoint Clinton president since she had won the popular vote, although losing in the Electoral College. A majority of Americans saw the federal institution that picked The Donald over Hillary as unconstitutional and unfair. (America is not an outright democracy where the people directly pick their national leader.) In states where Clinton lost by just a few thousand votes (especially where she was originally favored to win with heavy support), calls for recounts and election audits started to hit the airwaves.

Green Party candidate Dr. Jill Stein began a recount effort in late November focused on auditing election results in Wisconsin, Michigan, and Pennsylvania. Weeks of reports about Russian involvement worried Stein and liberal election monitors. They were concerned that the Russian government had potentially altered the outcome of the three "Blue Wall" states that swung to Trump in the final hours of November 8th. Stein raised millions of dollars during Thanksgiving weekend for an official recount in the three states, much to the chagrin of the Trump campaign and newly formed transition committee. Stein's team and a few other third party candidates considered potential future statewide efforts in Arizona and Florida.

Stein's team discovered photographs of damaged warranty seals on voting machines in Wisconsin. The company responsible for maintaining the ballot counting apparatuses countered suggestions of tampered equipment, pointing out that the seals in question were simply not replaced after routine maintenance. Nevertheless, the photos that quickly circled the web on social media only fueled anger amongst liberals. Unfortunately, before the fully paid for recount efforts could produce any evidence, they were shut down by legal injunctions brought by the Trump campaign. This shutdown effort left America with even more questions, especially about Trump's possible knowledge of nefarious election activities, and wondering where their money went. Thousands of liberal Americans, the majority having voted for Hillary Clinton, donated millions to the Stein recount fundraising campaign, realizing it might be their only hope in blocking a Trump presidency.

With the recount efforts stopped in their tracks, feelings of defeat finally swept the country as reality started to sink in. Many of us still believe – in fact, we know – that Love Trumps Hate! We've always celebrated the diversity of our country and have found the good in our neighbor regardless of our differences. We've always tried to find diplomatic solutions instead of militaristic bombing campaigns and baseless threats. We've always believed in the strength we gain from working together as opposed to the weakness of division. "America is", as Secretary Clinton pointed out, "great because America is good." If we lose sight of who we are and what we stand for, what do we have left?

During the discordant campaign, Donald Trump expressed the worse of America, while his opponent articulated the better side of a divided country. Trump demonstrated his glee in putting down the defenseless and railing against people who were different. He challenged, not just Secretary Clinton, but a large faction of the American people to stand against his unsubstantiated attacks on minorities, women, the disabled, veterans, and true heroes. He unknowingly built a formidable force in the people of the country he sought to lead, ready to stand against his dangerous plans and his future administration's policies that would threaten their rights.

Bullies shouldn't be presidents! Although America elected a man many disagree with, morally and politically, we owe it to the men and women who have died for our freedom to respect the peaceful transition of power. At the time, Trump appeared to have been legitimately elected to the presidency, compelling us to recognize that the will of the voters was for a Trump Administration to carry out a conservative agenda. Yet we must also remember that while Trump won the Electoral College, a surprise that still keeps a lot of us up at night, he lost the popular vote. The majority of Americans didn't want Donald Trump, his ideas, or his cronies to be anywhere near the seat of American political power.

Hillary Clinton, Tim Kaine, and the Stronger Together agenda were diversely supported across the country. Americans from every background, gender, sexual orientation, race, and socioeconomic class voted in favor of their collective vision for the country. One where every child would have the opportunity to live up to "his or her God-given potential". An America where the Basic Bargain was alive and well, where hard work paid off and our word meant something. Sixty-five million Americans voted for experience and tact, opposing incompetence and unfamiliarity. They voiced their desire to see an America that continued to embrace kindness and cooperation and where "Love Trumps Hate!" Yet their vote didn't put that progressive Stronger Together campaign over the finish line...even though Secretary Clinton walked away with the popular vote!

The loss in the Electoral College fueled a movement across America about the relevance of this antiquated institution – a discussion we'll need to have to change the course of recent events. More intriguing, in the weeks that followed the election, top lawyers and historians presented an unconventional approach to blocking Trump's inauguration and changing the outcome to match what a majority of Americas had indeed voted for. Several political organizations sprung up, focused on overturning Trump's victory in the Electoral College. One such group, the Hamilton Electors, challenged the prospect that the institution's electors needed to be loyal to how the states they represented voted. Similar to what had been attempted during the Republican Primary process, a targeted plan was created to flip electors from one candidate to the other before the Electoral College votes were counted and certified by a joint session of Congress. Faithless electors (those who stray from voting how their state has been called) have never changed the outcome of a presidential race. Even when last called upon during the tumultuous 2000 election, only one elector caused commotion, refusing to cast a vote for any candidate although obligated to support Democrat Al Gore. Nevertheless, organizers of the movement persisted, creating a massive letter campaign and cold call effort to encourage publicly identified electors to join the crusade and change their vote.

2016 was the year of the faithless elector. While the "vote your conscience" endeavor didn't change the minds of enough electors to override Trump's 306-232 advantage, the anti-Trump movement did create the single largest contingent of faithless electors. When Congress counted the results on December 19, seven electors voted against the candidates their state had supported. Two Trump and five Clinton pledged electors voted for other candidates bringing Trump's margin of victory to seventy-seven, 304-227. Former Secretary of State Colin Powell received three votes while Ohio Governor John Kasich, former Texas Representative Ron Paul, Vermont Senator Bernie Sanders, and South Dakota Native American activist Faith Spotted Eagle each received one vote. Former Hewlett Packard CEO Carly Fiorina, Green Party environmentalist Winona LaDuke, and Senators Maria Cantwell, Elizabeth Warren, and Susan Collins (Washington, Massachusetts, and Maine respectively) all received votes for Vice President. The effort wasn't strong enough to overturn the

Trump-Pence victory and Congress certified the pair as the winner of the acrimonious election.

Designed to stop unintelligent voters from picking un-vetted candidates for America's highest office, the Electoral College failed in 2016. Instead of supporting the most qualified, prepared, and experienced individual to ever seek the presidency, the Electoral College went for the antithesis. To add insult to the Electoral College failure, five of the faithless electors left Clinton for unfamiliar names. Instead of trying to whip support for Clinton, they picked individuals at random. The outdated presidential election safeguard proved it was broken when individuals like Faith Spotted Eagle and Winona LaDuke (as well as Senators Cantwell, Collins, and Warren) were given a vote having never been vetted by the American people or the press. The Electoral College was designed to make sure only the most qualified and formally investigated individuals took office, not to put largely unknown individuals into contention. The system clearly was/is broken, and after 2016, it's clear the Electoral College actually works against our democracy more than it reinforces it.

Ten weeks after the November 8th election, it was time for the peaceful transition of power to take place (a theoretical concept America is celebrated for). Inauguration Day, January 20th, 2017, was a day that most Americans will not remember. Unlike the Inaugural festivities that took place eight years earlier, few Americans tuned in to watch the 45th President of the United States take the oath of office on the steps of the United States Capitol Building. Even after two and a half months, Americans were still hurting from the campaign that culminated in Trump's election on November 8th. Others were just disgusted with a dictatorial bully being elevated to the American presidency.

Make America Stronger Together Again

On that cold January morning, after an awkward meet-and-greet with President and First Lady Obama at the White House, Donald Trump was inaugurated in the presence of his wife, children, family, and close friends. Former presidents Jimmy Carter and George W. Bush, along with their wives were also in attendance. Even though not obligated to attend, Hillary Clinton with her husband Bill joined the distinguished guests on the dais. Clinton later acknowledged that she and her husband (a Former First Family expected to be on stage) discussed with Carter and Bush how to get out of the ceremony that no one was eager to attend. Hillary's unobligated appearance gave credit to the authenticity of the Trump inauguration, legitimizing his victory and the country's peaceful transition of power. Standing just steps away from the former First Lady and Secretary of State, Trump took the solemn oath of office. With his left hand on his family's personal bible (stacked atop the Lincoln Bible held by his wife Melania), his right hand raised towards God, Donald recited the formal oath of office and was sworn in as the 45th President of the United States.

The usual aura of excitement was absent at Trump's inaugural ceremony. Unlike previous years, the inauguration was underattended. Instead of a massive, "unbelievable, (and) perhaps record-setting turnout" that Trump had foreshadowed, roughly 700,000 people showed up. In comparison, over 1.8 million people attended Barack Obama's 2009 inaugural. Even the generally crowded parade route, stretching from the U.S. Capitol to the White House, was sparsely watched along the city streets of Washington. Empty bleachers adjacent to the President's Parade Box were evident when cameras panned away from tight shots on the Trump and Pence families. Overall, the event lived up to its name (Uniquely American), as it was unlike any previous inauguration in American history.

A record-breaking $107 million was raised for the Trump Inaugural Ceremony and related festivities. While numerous events were set up, including a concert, it was bland when compared to the celebration eight years earlier. Unlike President Obama's first inaugural concert (where A-list celebrities like Bon Jovi, Beyoncé, Bruce Springsteen, Usher, and Stevie Wonder rocked the stage), the Trump Inauguration Committee was unable to book any top-tier talent. After the concert, donors and the general public wondered where all the millions went that had been raised. Obama's 2008 event cost less than five million dollars, while the Trump concert (unknown talent and all) had a price tag over $25 million. Unless all of the performers (who nearly outnumbered attendees) stayed at the Trump International Hotel, what happened to all the money?

Reported as a low attendance inaugural ceremony by the media, the Trump campaign, transition office, and administration countered that claim. They asserted Trump's swearing-in was, "the largest audience ever to witness an inauguration, period, both in person and around the globe". In the early days of Donald Trump's first month in office, the public debate with the White House over the crowd size became the top story. Reporters pressed the "largest audience" description over the policy decisions made in the first days of Trump's residency at 1600 Pennsylvania Avenue. When reporters contested the claim, Councilor to the President Kellyanne Conway defended the falsehood as an example of "alternative facts". Ultimately photographic comparisons, along with transit ridership and network viewership data of the Trump 2017 and Obama 2009/2013 Inaugurations, proved the new president's crowd was considerably smaller than attendance records of previous ceremonies. The Trump Administration, obsessed with size, couldn't compete with the actual record-breaking size of Obama's Inaugural. Had the roles been reversed, surely even Hillary Clinton would have had a record-breaking crowd attend her swearing in. With her popularity in the Washington DC Beltway, possible knack for email invites, and positive outlook for the future of the country, the crowd might have actually been the "largest ever".

CHAPTER TEN: ONE TERM – FOUR YEARS – 1461 DAYS

The Trump Administration, composed of former Republican National Committee staff, elitists, millionaires, and party outsiders, was unorganized from the beginning. Most previous administrations had pre-written policy and planned executive appointments that were an integral part of the campaign and expanded during the transition period. However, the Trump Administration only had a few cabinet appointees and executive orders in their pocket on day one. With inexperienced advisors and novice West Wing staffers, the Administration had a huge learning curve to get through before being in a position to start effectively governing. Within days, scandals and public protests against the new president added even more challenges to the already struggling White House.

The freshly seated Trump Administration was already spinning a fabricated story of record turnout for the swearing-in, parade, and fanfare of the inauguration. But the festivities of January 20th weren't just under attended; they were entirely absent of the energy and optimism of previous ceremonies. To add insult to injury, it will be the day after Trump's Inauguration that will be remembered for years to come. The new president's lackluster day and poorly attended inauguration was defeated just 24-hours later when millions of women took to the streets in protest of the new administration in the milestone Women's March. The movement brought out over six million people around the globe and the historic protests of the day will go down in infamy, leaving little room for mention of Trump's Inauguration in the history books.

The sheer disparity in crowd size between the Inauguration and the Women's March obliterated the weak voltage of the Administration's biggest day. Although Trump's team pushed back hard, trying to align themselves with the protesting crowds, the massive demonstrations consumed all the energy the White House expected to get after the Inauguration. Not only did it have a unique similarity to the 1964 March on Washington, but at least a million more people showed up – this time voicing disapproval for a stolen election, promising to stay involved in political discourse and vowing to oppose the sexism and bigotry central to the 2016 election of Donald Trump.

Americans, who disagreed with the outcome of the race and challenged the values of the new president, organized. Not only did they plan and attend the march on Washington to publicly protest Donald Trump's treatment of women, but crowds also filled streets, parks, and public spaces across the nation. (The Women's March on January 21st, 2017 was the largest single day of protest in American history with over four million Americans marching in solidarity across the country.) Women and men from every background, including many Republicans and political conservatives, joined in the protest against Donald Trump and made global headlines, driving a stake into the heart of a newly inaugurated administration. Although Trump once used the Twisted Sister hit *We're Not Gonna Take It* during his campaign (until the band demanded he stop using it), the words proved a better fit as the unofficial theme for the Women's March. For weeks, the protest made news, causing disruption in the White House Press Briefing Room and at water coolers across the country.

The first week turned out to be an even bigger disaster for the White House when suggestions of nepotism circled after the announcement of Trump's son-in-law as a Senior Advisor to the President. Jared Kushner, husband of Trump's eldest daughter Ivanka, was given an official position in the Administration after serving as a close confidant to his father-in-law during the campaign and playing an influential part in the transition process. Ivanka too appeared to be working directly on policy, which caused tension when she overlapped responsibilities typically reserved for the First Lady and other government officials. The implication that presidential policy was influenced by Jarvanka (a portmanteau of the couple's names) reignited questions of nepotism and political favoritism – last discussed when Hillary Clinton chaired a presidential task force on healthcare reform while her husband was president. (In February 2018, the pair lost their interim TS/SCI security clearance, appearing to push them out of an official position of political influence.)

Everywhere one turned, disfavor for the Trump Administration could be found. Few had hope that the new president and his shifting political message would be successful or make a difference for Americans other than the millionaire and billionaire class. Numerous cabinet officials had been announced and some already confirmed by the Senate, although few were welcomed by the people who dissented with Trump. The cabinet appointees who were seated were political neophytes, many completely unfamiliar with the departments they were tasked with running. Donald had promised during his campaign to "drain the swamp", but after getting elected he perniciously packed his cabinet with friends and cronies who were inexperienced in politics and unprepared to serve. As a result, disgruntled Americans became more involved in the political process, calling Senate offices and protesting at the U.S Capitol. Many challenged cabinet appointees, whom they saw as detrimental to the offices they were expected to serve.

The confirmation of former Texas Governor Rick Perry as Secretary of the Department of Energy was especially interesting given he had adamantly come out against the Department just four years prior. Did the president forget that on a debate stage during the 2012 Republican Primaries Perry pledged the Department of Energy would be "done away with" if he were elected? It also came to light during the confirmation process that Perry was unfamiliar with the role of Secretary of Energy; not realizing the Department administrator supervised the U.S. nuclear arsenal. Even a layman with merely a dial-up internet connection and desire to search through Wikipedia would know duties of DOE, under the auspices of the National Nuclear Security Administration, included managing American nuclear weapons and related facilities.

Appointee for Secretary of Education, Betsy DeVos, was an unexpected yet confirmed pick. During her Senate hearings, she defended guns in schools arguing that they provided protection from grizzly bears to schools in rural and backwoods environs. Tens of thousands protested DeVos' nomination and demonstrated in the Senate Committee chambers, at Senate "home state" offices, and on the steps of the U.S. Capitol. Teachers and parents were unapologetically in opposition to the nominee and denounced her background in private school, lack of experience, no involvement in the public school system (none of her family attended a public school), and her total support of school choice. In a 52-48 split in the U.S. Senate, two Republican Senators (Susan Collins, R-ME and Lisa Murkowski, R-AK) joined all of the Democrats (including the two Independents who frequently caucused with the Dems) leaving the DeVos confirmation tied at 50-50. Vice President Mike Pence broke the tie giving DeVos the majority. (Less than twenty days into the administration, the Vice President was required to break a tie, a Senate practice last needed in 2008 during the George W. Bush Administration and never used by Trump's predecessor, President Barack Obama.)

In addition to chaos surrounding the nominees and the eventual seating of Secretaries of Energy and Education, other cabinet appointees also drew heat from the American people and their U.S. Senators. Unlike James (Mad Dog) Mattis and John Kelly (the Secretaries for Defense and Homeland Security respectively), the majority of Trump's cabinet appointees were unable to assume office on Inauguration Day. Four months after Trump took the oath of office, his final top-tier cabinet appointee was seated, Robert Lighthizer, the U.S. Trade Representative.

Andrew Puzder, Trump's choice for Labor Secretary, dropped out of consideration in February of 2017 after rescheduling his confirmation hearings due to a known lack of support on Capitol Hill. Other cabinet appointees also dropped out before Senate confirmation. They include the nominees for Assistant Secretaries for the Departments of Education and Homeland Security, the Under Secretary of the Department of Agriculture, the Deputy Secretaries of Commerce and the Treasury, the General Councils of the Air Force and Army, the Secretaries of the Army and Navy, and the American Ambassador to Belgium. Later the Director of Strategic Communications at the National Security Council, Director of the Office of National Drug Control Policy, Deputy Administrator of the Federal Emergency Management Agency, Director of the Office of Personnel Management, and the White House Director of Communications also withdrew from consideration.

During the Administration's first few months in office, copious cabinet appointees were forced to resign. Others opted to leave their posts due to conflicts of interests, worries about the direction the White House was heading, or disagreements with Trump or his family. Notably was Trump's National Security Advisor, Retired General Michael Flynn, who was compelled to vacate his office in February 2017 (less than one month into his tenure) after communications between the General and Russia were unmasked by the press. The one-time surrogate on the campaign trail was also required to retroactively register as a foreign agent with the U.S Attorney General's Office. In addition to Flynn, the Administration saw a changing of hands in many key positions including the critical communication staff that is core to crafting an administration's message.

In March, Trump fired Preet Bharara, the U.S. Attorney for the Southern District of New York, and accepted the resignation of Katie Walsh, his Deputy Chief of Staff. In July, the Administration parted ways with several major players including Michael Dubke and Anthony Scaramucci (both White House Directors of Communications), Press Secretary Sean Spicer, and Chief of

Staff Reince Priebus. The following month saw the departure of Chief Strategist and Trump consigliere Steve Bannon as well as the Deputy Assistant to the President, Sebastian Gorka. In September, the first Department Secretary resigned – Health and Human Services Secretary Tom Price. He was forced to give notice after it came to light that he had spent millions of taxpayer dollars on private air travel for unofficial business.

Nearly once a week, new names were added to the growing register of top-tier staff shed from the Trump Administration. Many news anchors even began assembling comprehensive lists that by the winter (2017) were almost too large for the screen. News programs like *The Rachel Maddow Show* even had to group former administration officials together by job title on their list so Maddow could remain on camera, later expanding the wall of names by pulling out of tight camera shots and pushing the list around corners onto additional screens. In total: two Communications Directors, the Press Secretary, the Chief of Staff, Deputy Chief of Staff, Chief Strategist, Director of Oval Office Operations, Director of the Office of Public Liaison, Director of the Office of Government Ethics, and the Director of the FBI all left their coveted positions during the first eight months in office either by resignation or executive termination. (Many of Trump's closest staffers, including former senior employees at The Trump Organization, also left after Congressional and Special Council investigations appeared to get a little too close for comfort.)

The biggest bombshell, of course, was FBI Director James Comey's dismissal by the President, which brought the questions of collusion back into the spotlight. Trump fired Director Comey when he refused to pledge his loyalty to the president and end investigations into the Trump campaign, Russian involvement in the election, and former NSC Advisor Flynn. National Security Advisor Michael Flynn had been forced to resign because he lied to Vice President Pence (or so the Administration claims), but Comey was fired for a considerably more nefarious cause. According to initial reports from the White House, Trump fired Comey on the recommendation of his Attorney General (Jeff Sessions) and Assistant Attorney General (Rod Rosenstein) because of inappropriate conduct in the FBI's investigation into Hillary Clinton's emails. Later, the story would be revised as memos were leaked showing Trump's intent was to quash the investigation by the FBI into Russian interference in the 2016 campaign, an exploration that included the Trump family and Administration officials. Comey would testify in public before the Senate Select Committee on Intelligence for just 2 hours and 40 minutes in the summer of 2017. That testimony would become central to numerous investigations into the Trump-Russia collusion. On a side note, it's worth reminding that Hillary Clinton testified before the House Committee on Benghazi for 11 hours...a political ploy, not a serious investigation.

Comey's firing was controversial and became a blockbuster media story as parallels between the Trump Administration and the Nixon White House during Watergate began to emerge. The suggestion of potential recordings of conversations between Trump and Comey, made in a remarkable tweet by the president, had historians and reporters even more excited. In the Nixon/Watergate scandal, it was the recorded "tapes" of Oval Office conversations that finally decided Nixon's fate. Tapes have yet to trickle out of the White House, an entity that has become as leak-proof as a sieve with a gargantuan tear in the perforated mesh. If they exist though, it's only a matter of time before they are exposed – potentially becoming the pivotal catalyst in a politically toxic lynchpin with catastrophic Constitutional consequences. Perhaps it won't be tapes that sink this Administration, the transcriptions by White House stenographers may be enough to scuttle the Trump presidency.

While the Administration was having trouble appointing and keeping Cabinet and high-ranking government officials, it also was struggling to stay on message, arguably to create a message to begin with. After his inauguration, Donald Trump made calls to foreign heads of government (we can only guess how long it took for him to wrap his head around the fact that the Queen of England is the United Kingdom's head of state, not government). In a few early calls, Trump made threats to Mexico's President Peña Nieto over the construction and financial responsibility of a border wall between the two countries. He also yelled at Australia's Prime Minister Malcolm Turnbull over the Oceania ally's agreement with the United States under the previous administration to accept refugees. Trump ended up threatening Turnbull before slamming down the receiver of his Oval Office phone and abruptly ending the call to one of America's (seemingly former) closest allies.

Trump's problems with world leaders weren't, however, isolated to his initial phone calls with heads of state. The United Kingdom, America's strongest ally, debated on the floor of Parliament the decision by Prime Minister Theresa May to invite Trump to a state dinner. Many PMs didn't want this outrageous bully to enter their country. Replacing the United States at the helm, the French and German governments have taken over the role of "leader of the free world", advocating for the transparency and the progress previous American presidents of both parties championed. Furthermore, relations with North Korea tanked bringing America and the DPRK closer than ever to a nuclear exchange. In an interesting twist, the relationship with the Russian Federation that degraded heavily under the Obama Administration appears stronger than ever. Putin and Trump met numerous times during Donald's first twelve months in office, usually holding private discussions to prevent eavesdropping or leaks to the press. In fact, the American press often only learned of the meetings after Russian Television (RT) or the Kremlin broke the story. The alarming trend suggests the Russian Federation has at least messaging control over the White House...if not a tighter grip on America's president.

Executive orders overturning Obama Administration policies were among the only political victories in the first months. If Donald kept any campaign promises to his supporters, he did remain focused on dismantling the success of the Obama White House – even when it hurt Americans. From refusing to support programs like the DREAM Act (DACA) and the Children's Health Insurance Program (CHIP) to peeling off critical elements of the Affordable Care Act (Obamacare), Trump had mild conservative victories...though mostly all came from executive actions (EOs) instead of bipartisan Congressional deals. For a self-proclaimed expert negotiator and author of *The Art of the Deal*, Trump was considerably better at taking unilateral action than working with Democrats, let alone his own party on the Hill.

Legislatively, the Administration has had little success. Although at the start of his term the Republicans controlled the House of Representatives, the U.S. Senate, and the Executive Branch, the GOP has been blocked from passing major landmark legislation. Huge turnout among the American people to stand up for their rights have left the GOP with few options to pass legislation they desire, especially when many Republican Senators and Representatives face difficult reelection campaigns. The country has sent a message to Congress and the Administration: we're not interested in Trumped-up policies that only help the super rich!

One of the first failures to plague the GOP and the Trump Administration is the continued disappointment in passing healthcare reform. The Republicans in Congress had been plotting to repeal and replace the Patient Protection and Affordable Care Act (ACA), a signature Obama Administration policy, since they gained control of the Legislative Branch. Every effort was blocked under the Obama White House, but with a Republican in the Oval Office, it was expected to be smooth sailing. Most pundits expected the first legislative success of the new administration to be a "repeal and replace" bill, perhaps even with a presidential signature on Inauguration Day. Instead, the GOP didn't get close until the summer of 2017, only to have their efforts fall short after centrist Republicans stopped short of endorsing the proposal following mass protest.

The GOP didn't fare well in the fall of 2017 either, especially as the first elections in the Trump Pooh-Bah Era took place. Although final polls suggested key gubernatorial races in Virginia and New Jersey (along with the entire Virginia House of Delegates) were close, Democrats won big on Election Night. Unlike the events on that night in 2016, Election Day a year later gave Democrats a huge victory and momentum going into the midterms. Not only did Democrats hold onto control of the Virginia Governor's mansion, they flipped New Jersey, and gained seats in numerous mayoral races across the country. In the Virginia House of Delegates, the Democrats picked up 15 seats, bringing their 66-34 minority to a 49-49 tie...2 races being too close to call eventually went to Republicans. For many, Virginia was a bellwether state giving a possible glimpse at the potential for a massive annihilation of GOP incumbencies by Democrats in the 2018 Midterm Election. Others suggested that the state to watch for 2018 predictions was Alabama – which had a Special Election to replace Jeff Sessions' Senate Seat after the Senator was appointed as the U.S. Attorney General on December 12th.

With the failure to replace the Affordable Care Act (Obamacare) and the embarrassing hiccup in the 2017 elections, the GOP turned their attention to tax reform. Initially, they promised to hold open forums and work with Democrats towards a bipartisan bill. Instead, the Republican leadership took the debate over language in their proposal underground. In backroom negotiations, they developed an omnibus bill that would cut taxes on the wealthy while raising financial responsibility on the middle class. The bill, originally titled the Tax Cuts and Jobs Act of 2017, also cut healthcare funding provided to millions of Americans by a provision of the ACA. The legislation was meant to help tear down the previous administration's radical legislative victory, Obamacare, while passing the tax cut that GOP donors demanded.

The "GOP Tax Scam Bill", as Democrats and opponents colloquially referred to it, narrowly passed in the U.S. Senate after several re-writes. The draft passed in the House was dissimilar from the Senate proposal, requiring the two legislative bodies to reconcile differences on the bill. That process ultimately required the House to hold two more votes and the Senate needed a second vote in the early morning hours before a scheduled December recess. Although the Congressional Budget Office had scored the original piece of legislation and a few subsequent revisions, it failed to give an overview of the potential impact of the final bill. Handwritten scribbles in the margins were included in the passage of the Tax Code overhaul, but the long-term ramifications of the GOP's plan won't be clear until years in the future. Shortly before the holiday break of 2017, Trump signed the final bill into law.

The GOP Tax Bill was hailed as a huge victory for the Trump Administration. It was the only major bill to be signed during the first year of the president's term. Nevertheless, Republicans deemed the tax revamp a success, and the White House stepped in to take credit for the sole victory to date of the single-party-controlled government. Fortunately for the Senate Republicans, they got the bill through before their 52-48 majority dropped to the slim 51-49.

As the legislative discussion on tax reform was getting underway nationwide, in the deep red state of Alabama a whole different debate was taking place. Luther Strange, a Republican serving as Alabama's Attorney General, had been appointed by the governor to temporarily fill U.S. Attorney General Jeff Session's vacant seat. Well respected in the state, Strange immediately was a shoo-in for the GOP nomination to permanently replace Sessions. However, with the rise of former judge Roy Moore, backed by Trump's recently ousted Senior Advisor Steve Bannon, Strange lost the GOP primary and returned to DC as a lame duck senator.

The Alabama race caught the attention of the national news as Strange had been President Trump's pick to replace Sessions. Bannon's involvement also perked up the interest of pundits, recognizing that the man who once had Trump's ear now backed a different candidate than whom his former boss endorsed. Ultimately, Roy Moore became a national embarrassment for the Republican Party, much in the way Donald Trump had in the hours, days, and weeks after the release of the *Access Hollywood* October Surprise. Moore was publicly accused of having inappropriate relationships with underage girls including allegations of harassment, sexual assault, and statutory rape.

Moore was already considered a weak candidate after being removed from his position as Chief Justice of the Alabama Supreme Court in 2003. (The judge was dismissed after refusing a federal order to remove a statue of the Ten Commandments in a courthouse.) Moore later returned to the judiciary bench in 2013, only to be removed three years later for ethics violations. Once news of alleged sexual misconduct surfaced in his race against Democrat Doug Jones, polls in the state tanked for Moore and gave Democrats hope that their candidate, a former federal prosecutor, had a chance. Polls rose and fell before the race, ultimately suggesting a close contest with more than just a chance for a Jones victory. Low polling numbers scared many conventional Republicans with party leaders coming out against Moore and the behavior he was accused of. Mitt Romney and John McCain called for a replacement candidate, Arizona Senator Jeff Flake sent Doug Jones a check for $100 dollars, and the RNC and Senate GOP coffers stopped spending money on the race.

President Trump, on the other hand, doubled down his support for Moore having capitulated to Bannon, by delivering an endorsement for the judge after the primary battle concluded. The country waited, wondering if Alabama voters would support an alleged sexual assaulter like far-right voters across the country had in 2016 during the presidential election. Alabama's Special

U.S. Senate race was close, but by late evening Moore's lead waned and Jones took a winning advantage thanks to support in more liberal urban areas. Turns out Alabama wasn't prepared to send a child molester to DC, even if they were still supportive of the Bully-in-Chief as President. Huge minority turnout, especially among African American women, gave Jones the votes he needed to eke out a win...a political squeaker.

In the last 18 months, the State Department has been gutted like a mold-infested fixer-upper, with the framing damaged and the foundation cracked. It's imperative to America's national security and our foreign policy goals that we have a strong diplomatic corps, capable of negotiating our way out of conflict or preventing it from the start. In accordance with the Wilsonian (Woodrow Wilson) school of thought, the basis of world peace is the spreading of American values to every corner of the globe. American interests are best served by sharing our culture, ideals, and demands for democracy with the world – a task only possible through international development programs provided by the State Department. Having people in the field making connections is better than confronting the enemy on the battlefield. Diplomacy always trumps (pun intended) military intervention; communication is always better than bloodshed. From arbitrating nuclear agreements to navigating bilateral treaties to mediating a peace accord in the Middle East, progress in foreign policy can only be completed with a solid State Department. That is almost impossible to do with only a skeleton crew of diplomats and regional international experts. It takes career professionals with decades of experience, thousands of regional contacts, and personal relationships with local stakeholders to keep America on course. Without them, we're a ship deprived of a sail, lost in the windless seas of global chaos.

It's evident to foreign powers, allies and enemies alike, that the Trump Administration doesn't have a clue what they're doing on the world stage. Without a knowledge base of international relations at the immediate disposal of the president, mistakes have been made and our image has been tarnished. During his tenure, former Secretary of State Tillerson didn't always rely on the expertise of the State Department employees, choosing submission to thoughtless orders from the Oval instead. Meanwhile, foreign leaders like French President Macron are playing America's president like a cheap musical instrument. They've elicited Trump's ego with the pomp and circumstance of military spectacles and have accepted minor concessions in order to get him to genuflect in their presence. Noticeably these foreign heads of state have the last word, maintain the longest grip in highly publicized handshakes, and put their personal touch on bilateral diplomatic moments with power taps and dominant body language. It's easily recognizable that foreign leaders are exploiting Donald Trump's weaknesses to their benefit.

In his first year and a half, too many appointees and staffers left the Trump Administration to count. The revolving door at the State Department, where hundreds of career diplomats parted ways, was only matched by the torrid wave of executive appointees who dove for emergency exits after scandal, investigation, requests for unwavering loyalty, or repulsive ethical violations stemming from the Oval. Previous presidents had implied they expected loyalty from their cabinet secretaries, but Trump took a more obvious approach. Rather than sending up obscure smoke signals, he called out his political underlings on Twitter, to their face, and in front of the national media at rallies across the country. When he couldn't get an affirmative reply to his demands for allegiance, in true Donald J. Trump/*The Apprentice* fashion, he said, "you're fired". Well, actually he tweeted it or delegated the task to a subordinate, shunting the possibility of confrontation. High-level executive branch employees, like FBI Director James Comey and Secretary of State Rex Tillerson, found out they were fired only after seeing the words emblazoned on the chyron of Trump's safe space/co-president/biggest supporter, Fox News or after reading a 253 character Tweet.

Internationally Trump's successes for his first year were politically contentious. The Administration promoted a drastic shift in American foreign policy, announcing they planned on moving the U.S. Embassy in Israel. For decades, American presidents maintained that our diplomatic mission should remain in Tel Aviv instead of Jerusalem. Although Israel contends that the "Holy City" of Jerusalem is their sovereign capital, the international community has generally always recognized Tel Aviv as the Jewish State's seat of power. By announcing the change in policy, thousands in the Middle East sprang up in protest joining a host of international leaders in chiding the unilateral move that threatened peace talks between Israel and the Palestinian Authority. (Both states recognize Jerusalem as their capital, making the recognition by the United States a key point of contention.)

Ever since the final results were certified, Trump has had difficulty accepting his loss in the popular vote and public questions around the legitimacy of his Electoral College victory. At every avenue, he has drawn Hillary Clinton back into the political arena, even as she tried to fade into the woods. He took specific frustration when she published her tell-all narrative and turned

What Happened into a national bestseller. For Trump, the election was like a high school breakup and "Crooked Hillary" is the ex that he just can't seem to get over. Even the press can't move past the 2016 election, as after every scandal, every political debacle, and every presidential blunder, pundits publicly contemplate how Clinton would have handled the situation better.

Perhaps most damaging to the Make America Great Again effort was Trump's sliding approval rating which tanked almost immediately after assuming office. Due to his administration's inability to accomplish the many promises the president had campaigned for, win in state elections, or stay on message, right-wing America lost faith in Trump. Although Trump's core base of supporters will likely always back him, he lost support amongst the establishment conservatives and never gained any backing on the left. A *Quinnipiac* poll taken in April of 2017 identified the top ten words that came to mind when Americans were asked to think about Trump. Unfortunately for the president, those words were: strong, idiot, incompetent, liar, president, racist, leader, unqualified, a—hole, and arrogant. Some additional responses included clown, blowhard, crook, bully, moron, impeachment, and dangerous. By the end of Trump's first year, his approval rating hit a historic low, the modicum number less than any previous president since such statistics have been collected.

CHAPTER ELEVEN: THE BANKRUPTCY OF AN AMERICAN PRESIDENCY – RESTRUCTURING THE COUNTRY

The Trump presidency had an expiration date from the beginning. There is a constitutional limit to presidential terms and a greater humanistic limit to which we should allow a bully to tear apart our carefully crafted democracy. As the saying goes, "all good things come to an end", yet bad things hopefully end sooner than the good.

Although over sixty-five million Americans bemoaned the rise of Trumpism and the coronation of "The Donald" as the 45th President of the United States, it was a breath of fresh air for others. Millionaires, billionaires, the Kremlin, sexists, xenophobes, homophobes, chauvinists, isolationists, warmongers, white supremacists, and neo-Nazis all welcomed the Trump presidency. They were delighted with the America First, Russia Second, and "S—hole countries" last approach that Trump appeared to envision. They supported the tax plan that gave cuts to the top-earning Americans and large corporations while raising taxes on the middle class. More than anything, they supported the return of the era of intolerance and an unwritten policy that expanded the Jim Crow ideology to include the LGBTQ community, women, and anyone who wasn't Caucasian. They also rejoiced the departure of political correctness and professionalism from the White House, celebrating the return of an Andrew Jackson Era of brash behavior in America's Commander-in-Chief.

While the top one percent and Trump's supporters were overjoyed by his tenure, the Trump Administration has proving to be a bad thing for the majority of Americans. Bad for minorities, the LGBTQ community, and women; bad for education, science, and diplomacy; bad for the environment, our coastal ecosystem, forests, and national parklands; bad for states, our country, and the world. Like Trump's casinos, his term as president is in bankruptcy – deprived of political capital, absent of checks and balances, and intent to monopolize control of the FBI and the Judicial Branch of government. It's time for a reorganization of America, where power is returned to the people who built the country and distractions from prosperity are pushed aside.

Even before seated as Commander-in-Chief, the timeline for the Trump Era of American politics was fraught by the efforts of a massive investigation into the candidate. His campaign, numerous advisors, and foreign involvement by the Russian Federation have continued to be scrutinized by federal investigators. Everywhere you look, there is evidence of outside intervention in the 2016 election, generally paired with probable campaign collusion. Although the case may be a tough one to litigate in court, it's not terribly difficult to put two-and-two together or to make some logical sense on our own, outside of the judicial system. When we take a hard and fast look at the correlation between the 2016 candidates, the Russian Federation, various social media transactions, and a mammoth smear campaign, it's clear something went wrong...something happened.

In the early weeks of the Trump Administration, rumors from the campaign and transition period became a real concern for the new White House management. Every major media outlet, print and TV, started looking into the parallels between curious Russian meddling and the Trump campaign staff's behaviors, especially in the final months before Election Day. Consistently, the Rachel Maddows and Anderson Coopers of the news shared detailed reports of crossovers between activities by the Trump campaign and the Russian Federation's Main Intelligence Directorate – the GRU. A story started to emerge, quickly stealing oxygen from the Administration's initial activities and cabinet appointments. All eyes began to focus on the possibility of collusion, corruption, or even the outright theft of the election during the dark and divisive campaign from which the country is still recovering. Each new clue continues to connect the dots in a picture that is slowly coming into focus.

The Russian Federation (the successor of the Soviet Union – USSR) has spent billions of rubles, since the dissolution of the communist government, on a sizeable foreign policy program. One of the key resources in the Russian toolbox is an organized and highly sophisticated cyber-warfare apparatus that has provided a great deal of intelligence and helped facilitate the Russian Federation's foreign policy agenda around the globe. Starting back in 2007, Russian cyber-warfare programs began targeting foreign government servers in Estonia to retaliate against actions the

Kremlin dissented. Cyber targeting against countries and organizations that had become adversaries of the Kremlin continued through the end of the Bush Administration (2001-2009) and into the Obama Administration (2009-2017). Gaining momentum, Russian cyber-activity has persisted into the present, claiming electoral victories, embarrassing leaks, and destructive shutdowns in countries around the globe.

Following the Estonia case, Russia ramped up cyber activity and targeted the Georgian (country) government. Throughout the Russo-Georgian War, Russian intelligence groups hacked, externally removed data from, and took control of Georgian government servers. According to the United States Cyber Consequences Unit, a Beltway think tank, "the primary objective of the cyber campaign was to support the Russian invasion of Georgia". The Influence Campaign launched in Georgia was just one more example of the Kremlin's new plan to exert its power in Russia's geographical periphery and one day, perhaps reach its most powerful and detested enemy the United States of America.

The Obama Administration's response to Russian cyber-warfare in Europe was not very substantial. Attempting not to provoke or anger the Russians during an eight-year-long attempt at normalizing diplomatic relations, the Administration didn't put up a firm response. It has been postulated that American government officials put more weight on the desire to rekindle the Russo-American relationship than to address the injustices and cyber crimes being carried out by the Russian GRU and intelligence services.

In March of 2009, Hillary Clinton, then Secretary of State under the Obama Administration, attempted to reset the struggling relationship with the Russian Federation. The "Russian

Reset", as it came to be known, was designed to restore diplomatic ties with the Russian government that had been lost during the previous administration. Since 2008, Russo-American relations on the heels of the Georgia/Southern Ossetia incident of the same year had deteriorated substantially. The "reset" was a total failure in the long-term foreign policy goals of the Obama Administration, but it did allow for a brief softening of relations in the immediate aftermath of the "reset".

In the first year of the Obama Administration, the Russian Federation agreed to military concessions with the United States providing support for American air raids in Afghanistan. Both sides consented to reducing their nuclear stockpiles in an agreement similar to those agreed to under previous administrations. (A policy both governments seem to have forgotten.) In a further concession, so as to encourage more international cooperation, the Obama Administration canceled the George W. Bush Era plans to build a missile defense shield in Europe along Russia's western border. Planned for implementation in Poland, the shield had been a hotbed of controversy during the Bush Administration. The less hawkish President Obama dropped the plans to place missiles in Poland after Russia's President Dimitry Medvedev shared his concerns and plans to respond with a similar weapons deployment.

Many trace the 2016 cyber crimes directed at countering U.S. foreign and domestic policy by Russia to the accusation by Vladimir Putin that then-Secretary of State Clinton and the U.S. government interfered in the December 2011 Russian elections. Putin's party lost its overwhelming two-thirds constitutional majority in the Russian Duma; in fact, United Russia barely held on to a majority with just 49.32% of voter support. Putin's anger, holding the Obama Administration and Secretary Clinton responsible, is believed to have been the origin of an organized effort to counter the success of the American Democratic Party including the Obama Administration and the high probability of a Clinton run for the White House.

Over the course of the Obama years, relations with Russia degraded to an all-time low unparalleled since the Cold War. Russia began moving towards further annexation of former Soviet republics with American led opposition at every juncture. Russia set its eyes on the Ukraine, the Caucasus, and many other Eastern European states. They directed expansive cyber attacks at government systems and electoral mechanisms in order to put in place governments the Russians believed could be manipulated or controlled. The Kremlin's counterintelligence networks successfully rewrote the global agenda through strategic influence of regional leadership, putting pro-Putin loyalists in positions of incredible power.

In 2013, Edward Snowden, a cyber analyst for government contractor Booz Allen Hamilton, leaked our country's National Security Agency secrets to the media and accepted asylum in Russia. The Obama Administration demanded his return to the United States to face charges for espionage and disclosure of government documents, a request that went unanswered. The Snowden incident led to a further worsening of relations and an uptick in tensions between the two superpowers. Many believe, although it has never been corroborated, that Snowden gave details of American cybersecurity program vulnerabilities to the Kremlin. If such information were shared with Russian officials, it would likely have provided their intelligence networks with a clearer understanding of how to circumvent American firewalls and access secure government infrastructure and private business servers/networks.

The Russian GRU carried out a number of targeted cyber attacks against the United States during the Obama years focusing on critical infrastructure. Most of the incursions into the American infrastructure grids were immediately noticed and shut out. Unfortunately, similar attacks in the Ukraine went unaddressed leaving power grids vulnerable to blackout. The susceptibility of American and international networks to similar crippling has led to an increased question over the capabilities for the Russian Federation to carry out its foreign policy master plan, expand its sphere of influence, and regain Cold War Era parity with the United States.

Throughout the 2016 U.S. Presidential Elections, the United States claimed that Russian intelligence networks had carried out hacks on U.S. government servers, the Hillary for America campaign, and the Democratic Party's emails and fundraising arms. Overwhelming evidence was uncovered that many of the incursions continued for months during the lead up to the election of Donald Trump on November 8th, 2016. Conventional wisdom suggests his success at the ballot box was a direct result of information leaks and cyber hacks carried out by Russian intelligence networks with the goal of guaranteeing the Republican candidate's success.

As was alluded to previously, the Obama Administration had a minimal response to the cyber-warfare targeting of the United States and our foreign allies. While a number of economic sanctions were enforced against the Russian Federation, many consider the response to be a slap on the wrist. Each incursion of American networks was responded to by first fixing the cyber loopholes that allowed Russian access and second by implementing minor sanctions or making public dissent of the Kremlin's actions. The largest response came in the final months of the Obama Administration when a Republican Congress approved hardline sanctions against Russian foreign economic assets and trade networks.

Since Donald Trump assumed office, his administration has lapsed on imposing and enforcing the Congressionally approved punishments. As such, the sanctions are considered a failure of the Obama Administration whose handling of such a serious issue proved ineffective. Furthermore, the actions taken, both public and unknown to those outside of the government, have failed in preventing similar attacks in other countries. In the final days of the Obama Administration and during the first few months of the Trump Era, Russia breached French and German electoral processes and played a key role in the 2017 election cycles in both countries.

It is important to note, President Obama was very optimistic about the "Russian Reset" and had high hopes for close diplomatic and trade relations between the U.S. and Russia. Unfortunately, many within his government advisory circle were less optimistic. Secretary Clinton, Secretary of Defense Gates, and U.S. Ambassador to Russia Beyrle all expressed doubt in the "Reset". Each voiced concerns in working closely with the notoriously deceitful Russian Federation. In May of 2012, when Putin regained the presidency from Medvedev, Secretary Clinton shared concerns that the new Putin presidency might see the rise of anti-American rhetoric and a more nationalistic policy. She cited the questionable authenticity of Putin's election victory and the increasing autocratic methods he used to exercise control over

President Medvedev during Putin's tenure as Prime Minister. Clinton and Russian government experts at the U.S. State Department saw him as still fully in control of the government. He was likely calling the shots even after being forced out by term limits during the period of "tandemocracy" before switching roles with Medvedev. Her predictions have since proven to be correct.

Congressional investigations and reviews of Russian activities, especially cyber-warfare, have been conducted primarily in the House and Senate Foreign Relations and Intelligence Committees. On the whole, until attacks were directed at the U.S. Presidential Elections, little involvement was taken by Congress to consider the allegations of foul play by the Russians in other country's elections and their critical infrastructure grids. Congress did, however, express concerns that Russian invasions into Georgia and the Ukraine were unfounded and a clear example of the Kremlin's penchant for empire building.

At the onset of the Russian Reset, there was a clear cost savings for the U.S. as a newfound agreement with Russia allowed for easy passage of military equipment and personnel to Afghanistan. By traveling through Russian territory, the U.S. decreased the costs of cargo shipments into a region where active combat operations were underway, requiring a steady stream of resources. Additionally, by coming closer with an adversary, the U.S. had less need to build costly missile defense systems including the Eastern European Missile Shield. That system had been slated for implementation prior to the short rekindling of diplomatic relations. Unfortunately, as relations slid more towards opposition and mutual dissent, both the U.S. and Russia saw a military cost with armaments build up on both sides.

The cyber crimes committed by Russia also came at a geopolitical expense. Sanctions against Moscow for their involvement in the Ukrainian activities were imposed by the United States in March of 2014. Further measures were imposed in April of 2014 against a number of Russian businesses and oligarchs, especially petrochemical conglomerates like Rosneft and Gazprom, with the restrictions preventing commerce by those companies in U.S. territory. The European Union and the United States joined together to push further economic reprimands against Russian financial institutions, corporations, and government organizations under the direction of the European Bank in response to the Ukrainian Crisis. The final economic sanctions package that was imposed by the United States in the last days of the Obama Administration came in response to the Russian cyber involvement in the U.S. Elections. (Unbelievably, the Trump Administration later blocked sanctions nearly unanimously agreed to by a Republican Congress in response to the Kremlin's meddling in the 2016 presidential elections.)

The policy of the Obama Administration to publicly condemn Russian cyber-warfare and impose sanctions did not work in preventing such cyber programs from attacking American targets or other countries within the Russian government's sights. Unfortunately, the "Russian Reset" policy also failed as relations deteriorated over the course of Obama's eight years in the White House to a near historic low. In many regards, it is likely that policies of the Obama Administration led to Russia's push to impact the outcome of the U.S. Presidential Elections in 2016. By the time that both Secretary Clinton and Donald Trump announced their candidacies to become Obama's successor, it was clear Russia was obstinately opposed to a Clinton victory. Therefore, there appears to be credibility that due to disdain for Secretary Clinton and the desire to humiliate America while going unchecked in empire-building efforts, the Russian government – Putin – pushed hard to elect Donald Trump over Hillary Clinton.

Although details are still surfacing (likely for many years to come), Russia began to take actions to align themselves with the Trump – Make America Great Again – campaign. They focused on a candidate they could mold to fit the needs of their geopolitical agenda. By the summer of 2016, it was clear Russia was actively targeting the American electoral process, with a recognizable goal of helping one candidate over the other. Key political advisors and campaign staff communicated with Russians during the 2016 campaign, seeming to validate claims of Trump-Russian collusion.

For months during the campaign, stories had been circulating about Russian attempts to block Clinton's climb into the record books as the next President of the United States. It was clear to the U.S. Intelligence Community, all 17 military and civilian agencies, that Russia had their hand in America's election process. Questions had been raised even before the ballots were counted as to the legitimacy of an election with known Russian tampering. The Obama Administration allowed the election to continue, however, apparently hoping for the best and keeping their fingers crossed that Russia wouldn't successfully hack the election. When the result was so incredibly different than what most predicted, even more questions were raised. Had inaction by the Obama Administration allowed the Russians to seat the next president?

Wikileaks had released countless pages of stolen emails from the Democratic National Committee and Clinton Campaign Chairman John Podesta. The Russian government's fingerprints were all over the hacked emails and numerous other election surprises. Even the president-elect was questioned by the media for his role in the evident Russian interference, after the New Yorker made televised comments during the campaign asking Putin's intelligence services to release Secretary Clinton's emails. Every direction you turned, new inquiries were coming to light, most beginning to directly link Russia and Trump.

After the firing of FBI Director James Comey in May 2017, acting Attorney General Rod Rosenstein appointed former FBI Director Robert Mueller as Special Counsel to investigate the alleged ties between Russia and the Trump Campaign, along with the Russian meddling in the 2016 election, and the questionable basis of Comey's firing. The scope of the Mueller Special Council investigation was extended to any activities associated with election interference in 2016 or inappropriate coordination, communication, or collusion between Trump associates and the Russian Federation. Mueller engulfed several ongoing investigations including the FBI cases looking into former National Security Advisor General Mike Flynn, the Trump campaign, and the 2016 elections. That investigation quickly expanded, impaneled a Grand Jury, sent out subpoenas, interviewed witnesses, and issued indictments. As of May 2018, numerous individuals have been indicted by the Special Council: former National Security Advisor Flynn, former Campaign Chair Paul Manafort, Deputy Campaign Chairman Rick Gates, former Trump Campaign Aide George Papadopoulos, Dutch attorney Alex van der Zwaan, and Richard Pinedo. Mueller also indicted thirteen Russian citizens and three Russian entities. Flynn, Gates, and Papadopoulos all pled guilty and began cooperating with the Special Council – essentially they flipped to help Mueller with future indictments.

The Mueller probe into Donald Trump was made increasingly

more complicated by additional investigations into his family and inner circle. Trump Administration staff were also investigated by Inspectors General at each of the respective government departments for peccadillos on the job. From an opulent office dining room set costing taxpayers $31,000 and private Secret Service-style security, to a secure phone booth SCIF (Sensitive Compartmented Information Facility), and private plane flights to watch a solar eclipse and inspect the gold depository at Fort Knox. So much for Trump's promise of "draining the swamp"; instead he stocked it with money-hungry, elitist piranhas. They also posted pictures of themselves taking multiday Parisian layovers while on an official trip to Morocco and holding up big sheets of freshly printed money with a Scrooge McDuck smile.

Even Trump's personal attorney was heading toward legal purgatory when the FBI performed a no-knock raid on his office, hotel room, and home. Michael Cohen, Trump's "loyal fixer", walked right into the open arms of federal investigators. After drafting several poorly constructed nondisclosure agreements for candidate Trump, he too found himself in legal jeopardy. Cohen engineered several NDAs for women who alleged having affairs with Trump before the presidential campaign. Recognizing the critical potential for an extramarital affair scandal breaking before the election – beyond the rumors already floating – Cohen bought the silence of an adult film star, a Playboy model, and potentially other women who are purported to have had indecorous relationships with Trump. Those instruments of censorship are blatant violations of campaign finance laws as they possibly could have affected the outcome of the election to Trump's benefit.

A $130,000 payment from Cohen to porn-star Stormy Daniels (where Cohen claims to have used his own money without reimbursement by Trump or the campaign) would have exceeded the contribution limits and disclosure provisions of federal law. Under the statutes governing 2016 campaign contributions, any payment exceeding $2,700 would be a violation, one with damnatory consequences for Donald Trump, if he were aware of the payment or arranged for it to take place. Days after taking over as the President's chief counsel on matters pertaining to Russia, former New York Mayor Rudy Giuliani threw a wrench into the explanation for payments to Daniels. He claimed Trump was aware of the payments, had set up a system with Cohen to make similar payouts under a legally-questionable attorney retainer arrangement, and that there was nothing unusual to be seen. Trump later walked back Giuliani's comments, mudding the waters of a political scandal seemingly more serious than Watergate or the Lewinsky Affair. Regardless, it's a legal nightmare for Cohen who backed himself into a corner by publicly acknowledging the existence of the NDA. That admission effectively deemed the unsigned legal agreement between Donald Trump's alias David Dennison and Stormy Daniels null and void. That's $130,000 of someone's money down the drain. With the Mueller probe closing in on all ethical, legal, electoral, and financial considerations of Trump's campaign and presidency, Michael Cohen swiftly became the bone dangling in front of the President...just one more piece of bait intended to catch the big fish.

Central to the investigations, the Trump Troika – Jared Kushner, General Mike Flynn, and Carter Page – all had interactions with Russian nationals. They each communicated with Kremlin allies. Jared Kushner (Trump's son-in-law) attended a secret meeting with Russians at Trump Tower and attempted to set up backchannel communications networks for his father-in-law.

That apparatus would have been a conduit for "private" conversations between Trump and the Kremlin based at the Russian Embassy in Washington DC. Such a devious backdoor conversation reportedly never took place, although several exchanges between Trump Campaign, Transition, and Administration officials did continue. After taking office, Trump accepted numerous "private" meetings and phone calls with Russia's President Vladimir Putin, frequently avoiding normal procedure by speaking with Putin in the absence of American national security, diplomatic, or foreign policy experts.

National Security Advisor Mike Flynn, a close confidant to President Trump, had been forced to resign after it became clear that he had been communicating with high-level Russian officials. It is still unknown exactly what information passed through Flynn to the upper echelons of the Kremlin, but after just 24 days in office, a record low for his position, Flynn resigned. While General Flynn almost certainly violated the Logan Act, by negotiating with foreign governments outside of official American diplomatic channels, he became a central figure in the deeper investigation of conceivable collusion for his role in the Trump campaign – which itself is under scrutiny.

On December 1st, 2017, Ret. General Michael Flynn appeared in federal court to plead guilty to a single charge of lying to the FBI. As part of a plea bargain deal his legal team negotiated with Special Council Robert Mueller's team, Flynn acknowledged he purposefully misled federal investigators. He entered a guilty plea, admitting in a statement to "willfully and knowingly" making "false, fictitious and fraudulent statements" to federal law enforcement. The plea bargain acknowledged that Flynn became a part of Mueller's Investigation into allegations of Trump-Russia collusion and potential conflicts of interest, coordination with a foreign government, or obstruction of justice by Donald Trump.

In addition to the growing list of Trump associates linked to Russia, Carter Page (a former foreign-policy adviser to Trump's campaign) has been under scrutiny in numerous investigations. Page had frequent interactions with the Kremlin, with several trips made to Russia to discuss potentially lifting U.S. imposed sanctions while working for Trump's team. Special Council Mueller's investigators also flipped several former advisors and consultants of the Trump campaign and subsequent administration, to work on their behalf in collecting information on other persons of interest and complicit subjects.

Joining the pattern of Russian connections with the Trump team, numerous former advisors and campaign staff were also linked to the Kremlin. Paul Manafort, Trump's Campaign Chairman was found to have worked for a pro-Putin party in the Ukraine – a finding that required him to retroactively register as a foreign agent. As more details came to light about a $10 million dollar contract Manafort received in 2006 to promote Putin's agenda, the Special Council investigating the Trump-Russia ties indicted the former Campaign Chairman. Manafort was charged with conspiracy against the United States, conspiracy to launder money, and providing false and misleading statements among other allegations.

Every day, the Russian involvement in America's election became more and more evident. It's almost safe to say that Mr. Trump was not America's choice, but Russia's. While the investigation continues, it's critical that America not lose focus of the importance of the quandary we're in. In 2016, a foreign government seated our president, not the American people who were tasked with the obligation of picking the occupant of that highest held seat in the democracy we hold so dear. In standing by the wayside, we allowed our democratic republic to be outmaneuvered by the manipulation of an anti-proletarian dictatorial autocrat. We can never again let ourselves become as complacent or unconcerned with foreign involvement as we were in 2016 or the foundation of our democracy will ruin and our values will cease to exist.

In 2016 the Russian Federation attacked the United States of America, just as they have in other parts of the globe. They used the ignorance of a small fraction of the population, the anger and frustration of another faction, and the complacency of our nation as a whole to degrade our political process. They put their man in power over the other better-qualified candidates in both major parties. In 2016, the Russians conned the American political right, pulling off a maleficent deception executed with strategic finesse. Next time, the loser might not be the Democratic candidate, but the entirety of our democratic institution. Next time they might target the left, right, the political middle ground, or an entirely different sub-sect of the American populace.

According to the U.S. Intelligence Community and the Department of Homeland Security, Russian hackers compromised voting systems in at least twenty-one states. While there has yet to be any conclusive evidence of vote tampering, the hackers who penetrated state election systems assuredly had malicious intent. To say that intelligence gathering computer gurus from the Russian Federation would not corrupt voter databases after breaching their firewalls would be akin to bank robbers turning away from stacks of cash and bearer bonds after cutting the alarm, holding the tellers hostage, and safe-cracking the vault. It just doesn't make sense. In the case of a bank robbery, more questions would be asked. *Bloomberg News* expanded the count of states attacked by Russia to thirty-nine on June 13th, 2017 alleging that there was at least one occurrence of attempted deletion of voter data. If the Russians weren't looking to alter ballot tallies or adulterate voting systems, why did they penetrate U.S. election databases?

This is just one of the questions whose answer has yet to be unmasked in the Russian meddling investigation. It is crucial for the future of our country that we get to the bottom of what happened. We can't allow anything like this blatant theft of an American election to transpire ever again. Judging by previous examples of Russian election interference on the world stage, they're not going anywhere. Unless we solve the core issues that allowed Russia to coordinate and successfully disturb America's election, no country or political party is safe. Russia is not nearly done meddling in American elections – even worse, they're also targeting more vulnerable democracies, whose fragility will allow Russia to be even more successful in creating the global chaos the superpower desires.

In 2016, Russia released a massive, coordinated smear campaign to discredit Secretary Clinton and bolster support for Donald Trump. They used information that was tested and guaranteed to create unrest and unease amongst the American electorate. They crafted social media posts that took advantage of the least educated Americans and targeted the least informed, all the while helping to discredit legitimate sources for news and information.

Fake news posts, promoted by fictitious Facebook accounts, were responsible for the closeness of the election and potentially for the unexpected loss of Democratic candidates up and down the ballot. While the intrusion by the Russian Federation is no doubt responsible (at least in part) for Clinton's late night demise, alternative facts shared on social media platforms were the Kremlin's silver bullet. Clearly, many Americans get at least a portion of their news from Twitter and Facebook – these two social media sites are often the first and last things we look at each day. When the information shared on these mediums were outright lies, some Americans obtusely accepted what they read at face value. Unsuspecting conservative voters bought that a political novice like Donald Trump could "drain the swamp" of Washington elites and lead the gentrification of America like only a New York real estate developer could. An analysis by the *Washington Post* and a survey by the Ohio State University found 4% of President Obama's 2012 supporters bought the fake news stories they saw online and changed their voting behavior at the ballot box as a result. What's more, over 25% of Obama's supporters confirmed they had been tricked by at least one pro-Trump/anti-Clinton propaganda post promoted by Russia's Internet troll factory. That enterprise, the Internet Research Agency, was bankrolled by the Kremlin and later indicted by the Special Council, Robert Mueller.

Russian attacks against American voters were concentrated on building animosity towards establishment politics and abolishing the basis of qualified, experienced politicians. They crafted an argument in favor of an inexperienced outsider who would be seen as the proverbial "knight in shining armor" of the people. Russia engaged in a multifaceted collusion/hack of America's electoral process with the hopes of demolishing the foundations of our democracy. Although it has yet to be widely reported or discussed, Russia likely had its finger on the scales in the GOP Primary too.

In the history books, there will always be an asterisk next to Donald Trump's name noting the concerns over the legitimacy of his electoral victory. Regardless of the conclusion of all of the investigations into Russian meddling, the Trump campaign, the email hacking, and the 2016 election as a whole, it is undeniable that history would be vastly different had Russia not tipped the scale. The influence by a foreign government, to benefit one candidate and cost another, wasn't just unprecedented but was (and remains) inherently un-American and unacceptable. Trump's role in the Russian interference, while not necessarily criminal, is worthy of a special notation in the tomes of American political phenomena.

It likely will take decades for the entire story to surface, but after a year of the Trump Administration one thing is clear, Donald Trump was aware of Russian involvement at the time of their participation in the election. Collusion, rather poorly defined in legal journals, is incredibly hard to confirm or convict. Yet considering Trump's background, it wouldn't require as much evidence to prove coordination between Trump and Russia as it would another candidate accused of a similar act of cooperation. After all, Trump has a history of using other people and entities to accomplish his otherwise impossible to achieve ambitions.

Perhaps Russia's role in the 2016 Primary and General Elections was, in the eyes of Trump, no more unethical or criminal than his exploitation of Hyatt Hotels to secure funding for the Commodore Hotel or when he shafted Harrah's by refusing to build a parking structure until after the hotel company sold him their interest in Trump Plaza. Then again, perhaps Trump understood the Russian activities were illegal and corrupt...but just didn't care. He previously made millions cheating his workers out of owed payments, so why not cheat America out of the president they wanted. It's all in the art of the deal – you just have to persuade your audience into trusting what you want them to believe.

It's no secret that Donald Trump would be susceptible to extortion by the Russian Federation. He spent much of his adult life making shady business deals and cheating his way to the top. His propensity to speak his mind, uncensored, paired with his braggadocios playboy attitude put an obvious target on his back. As we would learn after the election, he even traveled to Moscow for a Miss Universe competition and stayed in the presidential suite at the Ritz Carlton. The suite overlooking the Kremlin and just mere steps from Red Square was notoriously "bugged" and monitored by Russian intelligence. A prime candidate for the industrious Russian Intelligence (FSB) to collect kompromat on, Trump would have effortlessly been played from the beginning, used as a pawn in the Kremlin's strategic game of geopolitical chess.

It would be remiss not to conclusively assert that Russia is responsible for Donald Trump's presidency. Without the meddling by the Kremlin in America's political process – a tactful use of computer hacking, promotion of anti-Clinton propaganda, election database corruption, and collusion with the Trump Campaign – Hillary Clinton would be the 45th President of the United States of America. Her campaign was poised for a decisive victory in the months leading up to the election, and it wasn't until the final hours of the race that evidence of Russia's conclusive and pivotal role materialized. Russia picked Obama's successor, not because they knew he would be good for the country, but they realized he could further their global agenda, destroy their enemy, and deal payback to the former Secretary of State that Putin detested and sought vengeance.

The Russian Influence Campaign is just one further example that America's democracy is not without flaws – weaknesses that must be addressed. The 2016 election wasn't the first time America chose a president, only to see a man that the majority didn't support take office. The 2000 Presidential Election between Texas Governor George W. Bush and Vice President Al Gore, often called the Election of the Century due to its significance and occurrence on the Millennium, didn't go smoothly either. Voter confusion at the ballot box led to numerous instances of mismarked ballots, late postmarked mail-in ballots, and the notorious "hanging chads". On Election Night, the too-close-to-call race originally went for Bush, but later became anyone's game. Close voter tallies on the morning after, just a 900-vote margin in favor of Bush in Florida, eventually spurred an automatic recount in the Sunshine State. The election ultimately came before the U.S. Supreme Court who decided the case for Florida, giving Bush the electoral votes that put him over the 270 threshold needed to win. Although Gore lost the Electoral Vote by four votes, he won the popular vote over Bush by 547,398. (This time around, Clinton earned a substantially greater victory in the popular vote – nearly 3,000,000 more votes than Donald Trump.)

At first, America put up a strong argument against the Electoral College. People disputed that the mechanism meant to protect America from electing the wrong man worked against the people. Sixteen years later, the same system blocked the first serious female candidate for president from winning the election after she too won the popular vote. Clinton walked away from the election with a commanding lead in the popular vote, only to fall short in the Electoral College – a direct result of Russian influences aimed at electing Donald Trump through the obsolete presidential selection apparatus. If left alone, the process that has failed the American people twice in the 21st Century and five times in our country's history will unquestionably do it again. We simply cannot afford to be duped again by an archaic constitutional rule that has no purpose or updated validation in modern America.

Americans must stand up for their right to choose the president they desire to lead the country forward. If our country is to be a democracy, then each vote nationwide should have the same value. The decision shouldn't be left to an antiquated system designed to prevent uneducated voters from electing a politically naïve candidate. After all, in 2016 the system guaranteed just the opposite of its objective. The electoral process, like the Constitution, was intended to change as the country grew. It's time we update the system and protect the future of our democracy in the process. A vote of the people to modify the law written in Article II and the 12th Amendment of the Constitution to abolish the Electoral College is of imminent necessity. The establishment of a popular vote (winner-take-all) system is the only way America can prevent the continued election of presidents not selected by the majority of the population.

The elimination of the Electoral College isn't the only safeguard crucial to preventing a repeat of 2016. Protections and safety measures regarding the influence of other countries or outside powers must be integrated into a more transparent and monitored voting system. The awesome power that comes with the American presidency must be met by a similar force constructed to watch over the activities surrounding the election of America's Commander-in-Chief. That operation should include third party monitoring, ensuring no elements within the country are actively working against the best interests of the people. America already champions global coalitions that supervise the impartiality of elections in volatile countries around the globe, why not employ such oversight right here at home?

Some have argued that we should hold a new election (immediately) to rehash the illegitimate 2016 result. Regardless of the potential collusion between Trump and Russia, a matter that will need to be prosecuted/litigated in court, the election WAS meddled in by Russia. They hijacked our presidential electoral process to guarantee a Trump victory. Add in the actions of Comey and sitting Congressional representatives who smeared Clinton's name – without cause – and it's fair to suggest the entire election was a sham.

Regrettably, even if America indicts Trump, Russia wins. If we impeach Trump or he resigns, Russia still wins. They still penetrated our free/fair elections, won a crusade against Clinton, and began destabilizing our democracy. If Vice President Mike Pence or another politician in the line of succession becomes president, the GOP wins. The only way to make this presidential fiasco fair would be a complete redo of the election. Or at least that's what some savvy political minds have suggested. After all, Americans did not pick Donald Trump on their own accord; they did it because of Russia and Republican smear tactics. Take those underhanded activities out of the equation and the reelection could be fair for both sides.

Perhaps in the future, when an election is questionable, we should install the Speaker of the House (or next available member of the Presidential Line of Succession) until we deem that it was a free and fair election, worthy of our democracy. Otherwise, the party that illegitimately wins gets the chance to appoint Supreme Court justices, rubber stamp one-sided legislation, and build a government of skewed partisans. There is no mechanism to reverse those actions, even if the legitimate leader was blocked from the role by a foreign power or a devious plan exercised by a political campaign.

Since the future of Russian involvement in American elections is guaranteed and their next target is of yet unknown, we must all work together to thwart their assured attacks on the horizon. Russian meddling helped the Republican Party in 2016, but the tampering of the American political process is not a partisan issue. This time Democrats were the ones who lost, but next time it might very well be the Republicans. Noticeably, Russia didn't help elect Trump to "Make America Great Again", in fact just the opposite. Their goal was to divide our country, an objective we can't allow to reiterate going forward. An adversary-procured bully intent on tearing us apart can't lead America. We need experienced leadership and a president who will put country first.

CHAPTER TWELVE: COUNTRY FIRST, EXPERIENCED LEADERSHIP

Every American has a place in government; every American has a voice to be heard. Our system of government is not about the president, Congress, or Senators; it's not even about our local elected representatives. No, our government is about you! The leaders who represent us in state capitals, Congress, and the White House may have different ideas, beliefs, and backgrounds, but they must share the vision for the future of America with the people of America. Our positions change, our beliefs change, our country changes, yet the foundation of our democracy will only remain strong so long as the American people remain invested in the political process, driving the conduit of policy towards change.

For too long, we've focused on politics only during the final hours of a major election. Instead, our involvement must be constant, always shaping the conversation and advocating for our beliefs. Our role is not to elect and sit back, but to vote, hold accountable, push/pull, motivate, and roll our sleeves up to help out. If the quarterback is the only player on the team, he'll never make a single completed pass. With a few players, he has a chance to pass for a reception, but with a strong offensive line ready to receive and an engaged defense protecting his flank, he just might make a perfect spiral pass for the touchdown. It takes a team to win the game.

While the voice of the people is the backbone of our republic, the American government was designed for elected representatives to carry out the will of their constituency. It is expected of these legislators, that they be passionate about the issues, experienced in achieving results, advocates of bold solutions, negotiators to reach common ground, and cognizant of their important role in the advance of reform, prosperity, and peace. America's political figures must be held accountable to the people they represent and the larger country they serve. It's as former Minnesota U.S. Senator Paul Wellstone always said, "Politics is not about power, about money, or about winning for the sake of winning, politics is about the improvement of people's lives."

Our government was never supposed to be led by elites and lifetime politicians, rather by the common man. Nevertheless, many of our greatest public servants have devoted their lives in service to our country. Through their experience, they have built credibility and the necessary skills to lead our country forward.

Our leaders should be experienced and should have a vision for America that goes beyond the present. Mayors can't learn on the job how to lead, governors can't learn in office how to respond to disasters, generals can't learn on the battlefield how to command troops, and presidents can't learn in the Oval Office how to steer our country towards progress. It is critical that we select the most qualified, experienced, and talented individuals to serve in our nation's highest office. At the very least we should demand of our presidents that they surround themselves with a team that makes up for any weaknesses.

During the 2008 presidential campaign, a first-term Senator took on a considerably more experienced field in the Democratic Primary and an unquestionably more experienced Senator in the General Election. Then-Senator Barack Obama had only served 2 years in the U.S. Senate when he announced his candidacy for President in 2007. His opponent on the right, Arizona senior Senator John McCain, had served in the U.S. Senate for over 20 years when he entered the 2008 race for the presidency. While Obama lacked the experience of McCain, he had unmatched passion and charisma that caught the attention of young and minority voters who usually stayed home on Election Day. When McCain pointed out the disproportionate experience between the two candidate's respective resumes, Obama responded with a clear strategy to make up for his disadvantage. Obama declared across the country that he would build the most experienced, most proficient, and most diverse cabinet in history. He promised to surround himself with political strategists who had been around the block, Washington insiders, and experts in their fields.

Obama won the 2008 Presidential Election because he inspired millions, put together an unbeatable team, and crafted a strong message. He also made an appeal as a presidential candidate who was so new to national politics that he didn't owe favors to anyone. Central to Obama's win was his argument to the American people that he would rely heavily on the incredibly experienced Senator Joe Biden, his Vice President, as well as a core group of political erudite wonks. For many voters who initially worried about Obama's inexperience, they were comforted knowing he had a team composed of the best people for the job, including Obama's former Democratic opponent Hillary Clinton as his administration's Secretary of State.

Obama's challenger in 2012 was an experienced Governor and businessman who made a name for himself as a leader in the corporate world and as a public servant in the political world. Mitt Romney had incredible knowledge of building a working coalition from his time as the President/CEO of the Salt Lake City Olympic Organizing Committee, as Governor of Massachusetts and as CEO of the successful private equity firm Bain Capital. Like Obama, Romney was well educated, more so than previous GOP nominee McCain, and had a great deal of executive experience under his belt. It was Romney's wealth of knowledge and leadership acumen that made him formidable in 2012 and drove the race to a four-point margin on Election Day.

After transitioning from a candidate to a president, our Commander-in-Chief is tasked with complicated enigmatic puzzles that only he or she can solve. It's easy to share a vision for change, but actually creating change in Washington is considerably more difficult. When Governor Mario Cuomo said politicians, "campaign in poetry but govern in prose", he was noting the difficulty of doing the job after getting elected. Unlike the euphoria of the campaign trail, the real work is hard and requires frequent compromise. Being president is more than just the pageantry of an inauguration or the clear answered predicaments illustrated in fictitious TV administrations. Beyond the photo-ops, press avails, campaign rallies, and Iowa State Fair soapbox speeches, the real work starts on day one when the president assumes the responsibility of protecting all 325+ million Americans. Unlike a reality show or a ribbon-cutting ceremony, the role of President of the United States is a serious job that demands a serious man or woman who is prepared to take the helm on day one and steer the country forward.

The issues that arrive on the president's desk require a unique touch to resolve. Easy tasks are not to be found in the Oval Office; the man or woman behind the desk must make complicated and often potentially catastrophic decisions. Reaching an answer on these tough challenges and hard choices requires more than just incredible experience; it requires humility, integrity, and recognition of the incredible power of the office. Only an experienced leader – one with strong connections on Capitol Hill will be able to push a legislative agenda through Congress and accomplish their campaign promises. Even though the Legislative Branch (the people's branch of government) was intended to be the most powerful, the White House wields incredible authority and a president must accept that responsibility without timidity for the corollaries of his/her actions.

American politics changed in 2016 when the Republican Party nominated the least experienced politician in modern history. The GOP's dark horse candidate, businessman Donald Trump, was the first major party candidate to never hold public office or have been an officer in the U.S. military. Trump had little background in the political world outside of contributing to candidates of both major parties and voicing opposition to sitting political figures. Although he won in the Electoral College, the majority of Americans voted for an experienced candidate whose resume was opposite Trump's and unparalleled in American electoral history.

Trump received an immersion lesson in presidential politics

"learning" how to be a politician on the campaign trail. He touted his ability to connect with the people and his stamina as strengths, directing both attributes against Hillary Clinton in the first Presidential Debate. He even criticized her for preparing for the debate. In a line that became a headline after their onstage sparring, Clinton retorted: "Donald just criticized me for preparing for this debate. And, yes, I did. Do you know what else I prepared for? I prepared to be president and I think that's a good thing!" Within seconds, Clinton's line was broadcast on the chyron of every network's debate coverage. Intellectual Americans enjoyed watching the highly qualified candidate tear apart the inexperienced GOP nominee.

Trump's naïveté in politics was clear during the campaign and even more so after he assumed office. Titanic blunders and consistent policy failures were the result of an under-qualified leader and an inadequately knowledgeable team. Experience matters, even bad experience, as failures allow for opportunities to learn and grow. Yet Trump's only knowledge base was reality TV and lawsuit-dominated business dealings that didn't translate to negotiation or diplomacy experience once he entered the Oval Office.

Donald Trump was an inferior candidate from the beginning and not just because of the ridiculous accusations he made or the frequent finger pointing and blame shifting. Never having held elected office or served in military rank, he was unprepared to run the country – he simply didn't have the background or understanding to be efficacious. While his contributions to society (at times gross and almost always selfish) were and are huge, he fell short of meeting the requirements we once expected of all our politicians. His devotion to his family and loyalty to his brand are admirable traits, but they by no means make up for his shortcomings in political preparation and geopolitical awareness. Trump's ignorance of American politics, let alone his mediocre understanding of U.S. history, put him at a great disadvantage from the beginning.

Moving past the turmoil of the 2016 elections and months that followed, we must demand that our leaders reflect the requirements of the office. As the highest and most important job title in the country, the President of the United States should be the best man/woman for the job. No Fortune 500 Company would seat a CEO absent a respectable background in an industry that proves the candidate's knowledge and leadership proficiency. The race for the White House, a large-scale executive recruitment competition, must be more than a popularity contest wagered between well-known or well-respected celebrities. Instead, prospective office-holders should have the performance track record, resume, and personality that merit the most prestigious boardroom – the Oval Office.

We can start by addressing how we select our leaders. America must break from the trend of repeating the same mistakes and hoping for a different outcome. We must analyze our errors and honestly attempt to recognize where we went off course. Then we need to work together to prevent the gaffes and miscalculations from continuing, or worse...repeating. We must acknowledge our errors, learn from them and find solutions that prevent their recurrence.

All presidential hopefuls must, at the very least, understand how our country operates and respect the institutions that have allowed the American Experiment to flourish and become the world's preeminent democracy. They must recognize the importance of history, learning from the successes and misfortunes of the men who came before – realizing that none have been perfect. The responsibility doesn't belong solely to presidential candidates though. It's up to all of us to hold our leaders, including the men and women who seek to replace them, accountable. Congress, political parties, and voters should guarantee that nominees and prospective political candidates meet the basic criteria history has proven will allow for success.

Although Article II of the U.S. Constitution only contains three eligibility requirements for presidents (one must be 35 years of age, a resident within the United States for 14 years, and a "natural born citizen"), we should expect more than these extraordinarily undeveloped criteria. All our leaders should be held to higher standards than the principal provisions of eligibility, just as any candidate for employment should be expected to meet and exceed the qualifications of a job description. A position of such reverence and importance deserves more than the basic requirement that aspirants have a pulse and carry an American birth certificate. Let Election 2016 be a lesson to any party in backing a potential candidate. Since a political nominee is in effect the one that is going to represent the platform and the character of the party, there should be high expectations. Perhaps each party will have to make their own written rules, but there ought to be definite requirements that define and qualify a person to be the leader of the free world, the occupant of the most prestigious chair on earth. In the case of the American presidency, potential office holders should be considered only if they meet the following standards:

1. **Experience in Public Service:** Presidential aspirants must have political experience in leadership and policy with a

track record of significant accomplishment that includes public service at the national level, in the military, or in statewide elected capacity. Presidents should be familiar with the expansive responsibility their office carries before they assume the job. A background of public service (even if only minimal) will ensure that a candidate has the training necessary to master negotiating, implementing policy, interacting with constituents, reacting to tragedy, and learning the pulse of the people that he/she represents. Understanding the job before entering the fishbowl environment of the American presidency (where you're expected to artfully engage with the press, tactfully react to tough questions, demonstrate your familiarity with policy, and understand how to work with friends and adversaries alike) is crucial to success from day one. An ice skater competing in the Olympics might be a good athlete, have an attractive costume, and a natural ability to captivate a crowd, but if they've never skated on ice, they won't perform well. Yet if they know how to throw a triple axel and have participated in competitions before, they'll have a better chance surviving under the pressure and putting together a program that displays their abilities. Like Olympic athletes, presidential hopefuls should go into the race knowing they have the skills to win a medal. Without experience in implementing an agenda (or even developing one), a president will be lost – failing to master procedure or understand protocol.

2. **Knowledge of American History:** Anyone putting his/her name into consideration for America's most prestigious job title should have an expansive understanding of the history

of America's highest political office, the country as a whole, and world affairs. They should appreciate the significance of the presidency, how to work with global heads of government, and how to operate effectively in the international community. They need to understand how to effectively lead the country, execute a policy agenda, and inspire Americans of all political backgrounds. Critically, a president must have a firm grasp on history, both U.S. history and more globally. Presidents can't learn on the job who the primary belligerents in WWII were; what led to the rise of the Taliban, Al-Qaeda, and ISIL; or why America's battle for quality-affordable healthcare is so quixotic.

3. **Humility in Service to Others:** Every challenger during the electoral process, especially the victor, needs to have humility and compassion. America is a democratic republic (really a constitutional federal representative republican democracy), not an autocracy, monarchy, aristocracy, or oligarchy. Elected representatives are beholden to the people and are expected to serve the masses, not their own interests. No man or woman is above the office, nor shall their power to create or block change be above the law or the will of the people who sent them to state capitals or Washington DC. Consequently, our leaders – especially our president – should be humble, respectful of others, and lead with kindness in their hearts. Unlike the dictators and royals elsewhere in the world, America's highest civil servant should direct our country towards a goal of shared prosperity, not singular fortune or personal gain.

4. **Integrity and Veracity:** No one should come close to the White House without clearly displaying his or her high

degree of integrity. The honor of serving in the Oval Office must be cemented in the truthfulness and character of the man or woman who sits behind the desk. Passion and persuasion are a given for a national leader, but honesty and integrity must be expected of any presidential aspirant. Voters should have no question of their president's intent, reliability, and incorruptibility. Fundamentally, no one should question the loyalty of a president – as his or her allegiance should never extend beyond America's borders or dissolve to less than every woman, man, and child that he or she represents.

5. **A Vision for America and the World:** Presidential hopefuls and officeholders should have a positive view of the country and an attainable, yet forward-looking vision for the nation. He or she should have a well-defined plan for leading the country, playing a central role in international affairs, and inspiring the next generation to continue to move America forward. That vision should put current times into the broader perspective of history and provide a clear-cut strategy for the future. Presidents should be able to explain in laymen's terms the benefits of their ideas, how their lofty ambitions would impact the lives of everyday Americans, and how their policies would benefit humanity as a whole. Perhaps most importantly, they should be openly documented so voters will understand how a president's agenda will be paid for and what each policy will cost taxpayers, corporations, or the national deficit.

6. **Strength and Emotionally Hardened:** Presidents deal with the hardest decisions of all. Often life or death, the situations that make it to the president's desk may not have

a right answer or a positive outcome. A POTUS must be willing to make the hard choices, have the courage to give unpopular commands, and accept the consequences of their directives. They will need incredible strength in times of unspeakable tragedy to manage local and global crises. As the nation's official Comforter-in-Chief, they will need the resolve to uplift a grief or disaster-stricken country while maintaining the muscle needed to lift America back to normal.

7. **A Distinct Presidential Look:** In addition to the important criteria regarding a president's knowledge and experience, a Commander-in-Chief must have the "presidential look". As the head of America's government, the President of the United States is our emissary to the world. What they say and do, how they act and treat others, even how they speak of our adversaries has global significance. Presidents must serve the country as best they can, which includes setting an example through appropriate attitude, rhetoric, and comportment. They should have exemplary communication skills and a mutually respectful relationship with the press. As our chief representative to the international community, our president must have clear and educated diction, always maintain professional/appropriate appearance, and never act as a bully or tyrant. More than just world powers and malevolent adversaries observe the president; American youth also watch what he or she does and listen to what is said.

Candidates seeking the American presidency and the enormous degree of accountability that comes with the job must be willing to meet or exceed these basic requirements. However, the fundamentals of experience, knowledge, humility, integrity, vision, and strength shouldn't be reserved only for presidential aspirants. Everyone seeking elected office should embrace these vital traits for public service and political appointees too should reflect these important leadership qualities. Perhaps most important in the process of selecting the next generation of American leaders, is a proper vetting process to ensure candidates don't carry damaging baggage like Donald Trump and Roy Moore did...long before they entered their respective races. Both parties can stymie future embarrassments if they look into every candidate immediately after they announce their intention to run. If contenders don't meet the standards above, the Democratic and Republican Parties should deny them from running on or for their respective tickets. As long as the candidate is not guilty of a crime, he or she could run for a third party nomination – as failure to meet the high standards outlined above would disqualify them from major party consideration.

The assignment is hard, demanding, and certainly not one to be sought by someone unwilling to devote him/herself completely to the service of the country, the greater good, and the desire for change in the world. A willing candidate will acquire incredible power and stature, but will also be burdened with unbelievable responsibility. He/she will often go without recognition for accomplishments and must be willing to give away credit to others for his/her successes, only to assume the liability of other's failures. We must run, vote for, and elect politicians who can meet these obligations – prerequisites determined by the ups and downs of history. Only then can we progress forward; only then can America generate change we can believe in.

CHAPTER THIRTEEN: CHANGE WE CAN BELIEVE IN

It's time to rise up, make our voices heard, and take back our government...one vote at a time. All of us have a place in America and each of us deserve a seat at the table. We all can be a part of the future we want for our cities, states, and country. We each should play a role in restoring America to the bastion of hope and land of opportunity it was designed to be. So let's get to work, let's roll our sleeves up, dig in, and break down the barriers holding us back. The Great American Experiment is a story less than half written; let's write the next chapter together!

Each morning when we wake up, we have a choice to make. The choice to get out of bed, to work hard, do our part, and to help one another out...or we can elect to sit on the sidelines, hoping others will do the hard work for us. Let's choose the former. When we work hard, stand by our principles, and fight for what's right, we can make a difference. By recognizing that we are stronger together, we take the first steps toward creating real change.

Our success as a country and as a people is measured by our

ability to reach across the aisle and work together, tackling the difficult elements that seek to divide or marginalize us. When we are divisive, argumentative, and pushing only one agenda, little is accomplished. Our country from the start was envisioned to be a collectively governed republic. The voice of the masses was intended to be heard in the halls of Congress since power was delegated to the people. Sadly, many Americans have sat on the sidelines for too long, letting a weighty few make the decisions for them.

We have always had faith in our federal government, even when presidential and congressional poll numbers reached historic lows. We've always believed that our leaders would do what was right and that they had our best intentions in mind. We have lost that faith; it's been torn away by years of votes supporting special interests over the desires of the people. We used to have confidence in our representatives to make educated decisions that would benefit our families and ourselves. Time and again, we've seen the pressure by firms along K Street and in corporate America take a front seat to the needs of struggling communities, crippling infrastructure, and striving entrepreneurs. It's time for our country to move beyond complacency...this is our time, so let's go and take it.

Every American has something to offer the political process in their community, even on a national scale. Everyone's talents can help promote the important causes we support; we just have to get started. It's that time now, time to roll our sleeves up and get to work. We actually can accomplish anything if we work together; we have so much to fight for, so much is on the line. Let's do it...let's get started.

To begin, let's make sure every American votes in every election. The responsibility of voting goes beyond just a constitutional right; it's an obligation. We are the only obstacles standing between the status quo and transforming our country to work for everyone. You can't complain if you don't vote, and you certainly can't make change if you don't share your voice.

Get involved in your community. Make an impact in your neighborhood, in your city, and in your county. Politics starts with the people in each precinct. You can make a big difference and cause a ripple effect with minimal exposure to politics just by getting invested in what is happening in your backyard. Make friends and meet your neighbors. Build new relationships and cultivate fresh conversations. Government doesn't always have to be divisive; working towards a common cause brings people together.

Challenge your elected leaders. Call out discrepancies and dissention with ideas you think are outside the vision for your town. We need your voice in city council meetings, state legislatures, and in the halls of Congress. Make your voice heard and share your story. Write letters, call Congressional representatives, and show up at town halls. Inspire a new way of looking at an issue with a personal account of how a policy has, is, or will affect you or someone you know. Push the limitations of partisan blinders by building bipartisanship on an issue too big for one group to tackle alone.

Politicians who are unaware of their constituent's needs can't make informed decisions without your input. Those with different viewpoints and open minds might be receptive to persuasion; others may find your perspective eye-opening, impelling them to frame an issue through a new lens. Believe in your role as a concerned citizen, as a public advocate, as a community organizer, or grassroots activist. You have the power – so go and take it. If you don't raise your hand, raise your voice, or raise your elected leaders' awareness, you'll never see change.

Find out who is running in your local elections and get to know them. Learn where they stand on an issue you care about. If you have common ground, join their campaign (on either side of the political divide) and get involved in the discussion. Help them shape a strong platform that orientates the community towards progress. Be a sounding board and give advice, there's always a need for fresh opinions. Use your experience to connect with voters in new and innovative ways, utilizing out of the box ideas to increase your candidate's broad-base appeal.

Lend a hand however you can; candidates need all the support they can get. Bake cookies for the staff, prepare a healthy lunch for organizers, or brew the coffee for campaign headquarters. Even the little stuff means a lot. An extra drop of caffeine or energy is all some need to make one more call, knock on one more door, or secure one more vote. All it takes is an ounce of compassion to create a gallon of goodness.

Hit the streets and organize, campaign, and advocate for what is important to you. Rally support for the ballot measures, policies, and candidates you endorse, encouraging others to get involved too. Share with your friends, family, and neighbors what a measure is about or what your candidate stands for. Convince them to join the effort, then team up and spread the word even further. Grassroots advocacy works because it puts a face behind the message. Door-to-door politics allows people to have important one-on-one discussions, giving you the opportunity to flip someone who maybe didn't support a measure or politician before.

Staff campaign events, spin the campaign narrative to local

press, and help craft a message for success. The more you get involved, the more you'll learn. The more you learn, the more valuable you are to the process and the more likely you'll be successful in advancing a candidate, agenda, or ballot proposal. Even the least experienced and first-time volunteers can quickly rise in the ranks of a campaign. If you have the drive, ambition, and tenacity, you can make an incredible impact.

Canvass, phone bank, fold mailers, build social media presence, and connect with likely voters. This is crucial, especially in states where retail politics (connecting with voters intimately) is key to winning. Most state and local elections are composed of largely unknown candidates. Going door-to-door and having in-person exchanges is essential to explain what your movement entails and who your candidate is. Connect with voters in every way you can. Hand out leaflets, knock doors, and make calls. Even if you're shy or reserved, you can make a difference. Each door and every call will bolster your confidence and build your public speaking competences. If you take nothing else away from a campaign, you'll have stronger communication proficiencies that will enhance your resume and help you for the rest of your life...and on your next campaign.

Not everyone wants to be involved in the political spin or campaign activities. Not to worry, there are plenty of other critical functions that help our political process. Drive people to the polls. Volunteer at Primaries, Caucuses, and General Election polling places – where you can't persuade voters. Help out at the ballot box. Polling places always need monitors, judges, and set-up volunteers. There's also probably a need for translators at voting locations near you. Don't let a language barrier prevent someone from casting their vote and making their voice heard. Study up on key terms, phrases, and campaign specifics in the language(s) you speak so you can explain to voters who need a translation of rules, criteria, or candidate/ballot measure details. (Just remember it's not legal to push the partisanship while you're working at the polling place...in the car, driving voters to the ballot box on the other hand is free game.)

Want to make an even bigger impact? Believe in our country, believe in yourself, and inspire others to believe in you by running for office. If your community leadership needs a new face or a new agenda, put your name in contention. Lend your experiences and background to your community and run for office yourself. Experience doesn't need to come from law school, years in the military, or decades in the walls of a Capitol Building. It's composed of mothers, fathers, teachers, farmers, and businessmen, all who have broad experience. College graduates, fishermen, salesmen, and spiritual leaders, all have experience too. It's up to all of us, to use our skills, our knowledge, and our strengths to write the future of America. We all have something unique to offer; we all have a role to play. For some of us, our talents are best suited for standing behind the podium as the candidate. Try it for yourself, who knows, maybe you are meant to be a public servant.

Remember the presidential elections in 2016, a complete stranger to politics won on the biggest stage in America. If you're already involved in the public debate, already lending your voice on key issues, and have a bit of experience under your belt, you too could win big. Many races in America, especially at the local/state level, go uncontested as no one primaries or challenges incumbents and strong candidates. Don't be held back by the prospect of defeat, oppose those incumbencies and put your name into consideration. Perhaps the addition of a new voice, a new face, and a new perspective will influence voters to try a new leader – you!

Take a leap of faith, put yourself out there, and build a base to tackle the issues you see need to be addressed. Debate the field and push for your positions. Drive the conversation towards what matters most to your constituency and away from the nonsensical trivia that bogs down political races. Then win or lose at the ballot box, keep fighting for the change you want to see.

We unquestionably should require every high school student across America to get involved in the political process, especially in a Midterm or Presidential Election year. So many of our country's youth go unheard in political campaigns, so few get involved in the movement to elect the leaders who decide their future. Getting an early glimpse at political coordination up close will help shape the next generation of American politicians, activists, and organizers. The responsibility rests in the hands of America's politicians to inspire our youth to get involved, become socially aware, and play a part in our government.

I remember my first campaign. In high school during the 2008 Presidential Elections, I read as much as I could and watched the debates. My ideals were aligned with the Clinton campaign. However, after her loss to Obama in the Democratic Primary, I became an Obama defender. I even remember monitoring races on Election Days prior to that. It wasn't until I went to college that I became active in the political process. I knocked doors, made cold calls, and talked to voters on the streets. I raised social awareness and made an impact in my community, often getting commitments from likely-voters whom I had a discussion with. It was challenging, inspiring, and I felt successful when I changed a voter's mind.

Ever since that first election, I ramped up my involvement. From knocking on doors and campaigning for state and federal elections to traveling the country and even considering a run myself – the experience has been amazing. Every American student should have the same opportunity; maybe some will even run for an office after getting a taste of politics. I know that our next leaders, America's youth, are ready to play their part in the political process because they believe in America.

CHAPTER FOURTEEN: BELIEVE IN AMERICA

We've been knocked down – for some by the historic loss of a presidential contest, for others by the divisions we see in our community. However, we can't give up on the promise of America, on our friends and neighbors, on our partisan adversaries, or our political process. President Bill Clinton said of times like these, "If you live long enough, you'll make mistakes. But if you learn from them, you'll be a better person. It's how you handle adversity, not how it affects you. The main thing is never quit, never quit, never quit." So, let's learn from our mistakes in 2016, take the advice of our 42nd President, and make sure we never slip back to such a divisive and ugly place ever again. Maybe we can find a way to "Believe in America" once more and get past the differences that separate us.

Our country has withstood numerous challenges that sought to divide us and destroy the foundations of our democracy. We've withstood wars with foreign powers and attacks by enemies within our own borders. We watched as brothers took up arms against brothers in the streets of America and on the Civil War battlefields. We've weathered depressions, recessions, and clawed our way out of economic downturns. We watched our neighbors get thrown out of our communities because they're different, and we fought cyclical proxy wars in Korea and Vietnam. Through all these trials, we've found ways to come together as a nation, to find the good in our fellow citizens, and to look toward the future we want to build together.

Our country wasn't built overnight. America was constructed on the backs of millions of Americans. Those framers of our modern democratic republic fought opposition from all sides, creating a country without comparison. In our darkest hours, we were one – one nation, one people. Our successes are the result of collective work over centuries and the culmination of collaboration, cooperation, and coordination of many hands building a nation together.

President Obama often said during the 2012 General Election, that one individual didn't build America by his or herself. Obama contested Governor Mitt Romney's self-determination attitudes, arguing that while our drive and hard work help make us successful, our triumph is rooted in working together. In what became a key point in his reelection campaign, Obama defended his argument, suggesting:

"If you've been successful, you didn't get there on your own. I'm always struck by people who think, well, it must be because I was just so smart. There are a lot of smart people out there. It must be because I worked harder than everybody else. There are a whole bunch of hardworking people out there. If you were successful, somebody along the line gave you some help. There was a great teacher somewhere in your life. Somebody helped to create this unbelievable American system that we have that

Make America Stronger Together Again

allowed you to thrive. Somebody invested in roads and bridges. If you've got a business — you didn't build that. Somebody else made that happen. The Internet didn't get invented on its own. Government research created the Internet so that all the companies could make money off the Internet. The point is, is that when we succeed, we succeed because of our individual initiative, but also because we do things together."

–Barack Obama, Campaign Speech, July 13, 2012, Roanoke Virginia

President Obama was right; America wasn't built by our individual initiative alone, but by our collective advocacy and shared efforts. It's time to get back to work, building a better America together. It's time to commit ourselves to fight for the values, principles, initiatives, policies, and candidates we support. As the legendary Jimmy Valvano once said, "every single day, in every walk of life, ordinary people do extraordinary things." People have the power to make incredible change, so long as they believe in themselves, what they're fighting for, and what they can accomplish by working with others.

Valvano, an American basketball icon, inspired the teams he coached, giving them words of motivation and a clear picture of victory. In 1983, his North Carolina State University team won the national title, against all odds. But Valvano's team wasn't the last to break all odds. Barack Obama became the first African American president, Hillary Clinton became the first woman to lead a major American political party, and countless Americans have made an impact in their communities, helping to bring change to every corner of the country. Future generations will break through their own barriers, explore their own new frontiers, and discover the amazing capacity they have to change the world.

Since the election in 2016 and the subsequent inauguration of

Donald Trump, a wave of Americans stepped up and became more involved in the political process. They've marched against hate, called on U.S. Senators to protect healthcare, defended American values, ran for office themselves, and improved their neighborhoods. Together they worked hard focusing on making change. They put in the extra effort not because they had to, but because they understood it was the right thing to do – because they believed in America.

Americans, especially millennials, are just now starting to see their potential. They are ready to move our country forward. Thanks to the incredibly low turnout of the 2016 election, Americans of all backgrounds, young and old, are coming out of the woodwork and getting engaged in politics. They're standing up for what they support and letting their representatives know we all still deserve a say in the future of America. Most importantly, they are paying attention...closely watching what Congress and the White House do and reacting every step of the way. No longer are people sitting on the bench, they're getting into the game, playing hard, and claiming small victories right and left.

Getting back on track and becoming stronger together is a noble goal, yet we have a long way to go and we're nowhere near finished. America has taken giant steps backward since Donald Trump came onto the political field. We've lost touch of who we are and what we stand for. Still, America didn't become the leader of the free world overnight and one man won't bring our country down on his own. Instead, the experiences we faced in 2016 and the days since, will harden us as we press onward – together.

As a nation, we've grown apart, more divided than nearly any other time in our history. Nevertheless, in some circles, we've also grown closer – 2016 gave us a common visceral instinct to get involved in the political space often participated in by just a few. We've shown how we can come together – winning victories in elections since Trump's upset in 2016 and procuring wins against damaging legislation. But will it be enough? Will we keep moving forward or will the momentum die a classic death of hopelessness? So long as we continue working together, we can return to being successful as a country and perhaps stave off Trump's populist political rise that threatens the very fabric of our democracy.

In order to move forward, however, we have to go beyond just believing in America. We have to believe in the truth. Too many across our county are lost in the weeds of confusion; too many are ill-informed. For decades we've struggled with a domestic education failure, where the least educated amongst us are led to believe untrue and biased "alternative facts". They've naively been led to trust that political spin from one side is the truth and counterarguments are lies. We should be able to put the facts first and the political bias second. While you're entitled to your own opinion, you're not entitled to your own facts. America has slowly become a society where implicit bias and uninformed voters take newscasters, social media posts, and op-eds at their word. We've failed ourselves by accepting what we see and hear without fact-checking it for ourselves. As a result, we drift apart.

In fact, we've crowded into corners, refusing to listen to ideas or views different than our own. Like baby chicks (who are kept in enclosures with curved edges to prevent lethal smashups in square boxes), we run immediately away from our political opponents. At the slightest hint of political debate, we rush to our familiar corners (Left/Right, Democrat/Republican), seeking the security of our peers (power in numbers). Unfortunately, we're unknowingly crushing ourselves to death just like the baby chicks. Instead of heading towards the middle ground and interacting (listening/learning) with those from the other side, we're comfortable dying in our corner. (Baby chicks run toward the corners, huddling together to stay warm by utilizing their collective body heat. If they all grouped together in the middle, away from the corners, the chicks would stay warm and none would be crushed to death.) We too can prevent America from being defeated by choosing to head for the middle ground, listen to each other, and work together instead of crumpling up in our partisan corners. We mustn't be foolish like baby chicks and let our democracy die.

While we're divided down the middle, opting for the safety of our respective corners, Americans aren't all that different. Most of us want to do what's best for our families, communities, states, and our country. We want to live a better, safer, fuller life. We want to make sure no one gets left behind, left out, or altogether forgotten. However, these goals are only attainable if we get past the partisan blinders that bar us from seeing the benefits of cooperation. (Bipartisanship was the vision of America's founders and it was preserved as the basis of our democracy by the framers of the Constitution.) We mustn't tune out or block the views of others, even if they seem entirely opposite of what we believe. Our political diversity, like our diversity in race, religion, gender, and sexual orientation, should make us stronger. Differences in opinion give us a greater insight on important issues and a unique perspective that we might miss if they go unheard.

Since Donald Trump entered the race for president, blasting minorities, people with disabilities, women, and anyone whom he disliked, we've changed. We're not the same anymore. It might be hard to believe some of us are actually better off after a divisive election that left the country split down the middle, angry, and resistant to collaboration. Just as the threat of Nazism and communism inspired the West to break barriers, fend off hate, and push back...MAGA has given America a new adversary. The Make America Great Again agenda has given many us a new force for conscription, bringing new and increasingly liberal faces into the ranks of the politically invested. Hopefully, we're coming together as a nation, Republican and Democrat, to stand up for affordable healthcare, to stop corruption by administration officials, and to demand more from our leaders. Even a few GOP Congressional representatives, conservative pundits, and lifelong card-carrying Republicans have refused to run on, defend, or support the Trump agenda.

In recent years, the recognition that we have more that unites us than divides us was no clearer than at the 2012 Al Smith Memorial Foundation Dinner. At the event, President Obama and Republican candidate Mitt Romney exchanged pleasantries in their comical speeches signifying the importance of humanity over partisan politics. In his address from the dais, Romney said, "We have very fundamental and sound principles that guide both the president and me. It'd be easy to let a healthy competition give way to the personal and the petty but fortunately, we don't carry the burden of disliking one another...In our country, you can oppose someone in politics and make a confident case against their policies without any ill-will...There is more to life than politics." President Obama shared the sentiment, noting "We may have different political perspectives, but I think – in fact, I'm certain – that we share the hope that the next four years will reflect the same decency and the same willingness to come together for a higher purpose that are on display this evening."

For most of us, the disgusting and vile behavior from Donald Trump's past, known to most before the election, is no longer acceptable. Women and men nationwide are standing up against chauvinist leaders in nearly every industry, sparking the #MeToo movement. We've demanded the resignations of corporate chiefs, media moguls, and politicians. We've shamed the imbalanced gender representation in movies, TV, the business world, and politics. We've found the strength to share our stories of abuse, assault, and mistreatment – tearing the power away from those who tried to silence us. We've exercised our constitutional rights, insisting that our voices be heard and our concerns addressed. Perhaps Donald Trump and his rancorous MAGA agenda have instigated the momentum in this climate of change.

The new normal that pundits discussed in the aftermath of Trump's unexpected emergence as the GOP nominee, and later president, now includes increased participation by a previously untapped segment of the American electorate. We've now started to pay attention to what's happening in Washington DC and how our representatives are voting. We've also started to push back – demanding that our voices be heard and our questions be answered. We're in touch with our government in a way we've never been before, more aware of the consequences of our votes and the power of our numbers.

We are all part of the future of our county; we can all have a place in the political leadership of America. Democrats have clear frontrunners in Chris Murphy, Cory Booker, and Kamala Harris. Republicans have clear leaders too – Mitt Romney, Jeff Flake, and John Kasich. While one of these named figures will no doubt derail the Trump Train, they are only the immediate leaders of America. The future of the country lies in our hands. A future president, no doubt, rests amongst us – not to be denied of his/her chance at serving in that high office and making change.

The hope and change that sparked the movement leading to the inauguration of the first African American president is not dead...it's not gone. That passion still exists in the American spirit. Even though it didn't make an appearance in 2016, it's still a part of who we are. The message of hope and change shouldn't be a focus just in election years, but rather a constant part of our lives, a way of living – even a vision for the future. Just imagine what we are capable of collectively if we return to being hopeful, optimistic for change, and ready to move forward.

CHAPTER FIFTEEN: FORWARD

The future of our country will be decided by those who have the initiative to work and fight for an inclusive America; those who have the fortitude to stay true to the values and principles our nation was founded upon; and those who have the courage to risk everything to build a bright and prosperous future for the country they love! Ronald Reagan famously said, "Freedom is only one generation away from extinction." It's up to all of us to protect the liberties and freedoms our country guarantees and pass them on to future generations of Americans.

Our nation is a government of, by, and for the people with opportunities for success and achievement made available to all. Regardless of who you are, where you're from, what you look like, whom you love, what you believe, or how you vote, our government has an obligation to work and fight for all of us! We all have the duty to demand with our vote that the leaders we elect represent us (the people) and not the special interests, multinational corporations, foreign adversaries, or the agenda of a single political party. Our president has a prescriptive responsibility to represent the people, all of us, regardless of our party affiliation. While we've always believed that our best days are yet to come, in light of the divisive 2016 election we've come to question whether those days have already passed. Always the optimist, I know our finest hour still lies ahead, our full potential is still untapped, and our desire to live up to the American Dream is stronger than ever. While we haven't reached that point yet, advocating for the following reforms will bring us closer to an electoral system that works for everyone.

Evening the Odds/ Money In Politics

Our first step should be to even the odds by taking dark money out of politics and making elections more economical. In 2016, the money spent on the presidential elections alone exceeded $2.38 billion dollars. A total of $6.4 billion was expended in the Primary and General Elections from city council to the White House. Think of all the causes that would have made better use of that money than the thousands of attack ads, millions of social media posts, and countless detestable television commercials. While a considerable amount was raised by individual campaigns, most of the expenditures came from big Political Action Committees (PACs) and Super PACs.

Campaign finance reform is crucial to leveling the playing field to prevent today's millionaires and billionaires from using the stranglehold of their financial capabilities to wield political power. As long as the wealthiest Americans can funnel money to candidates in exchange for their votes, policy will never work in the interests of all Americans. Instead the wealthy will grow richer, the poor will get poorer, and the middle class will be wiped out altogether.

That is only the beginning. So long as corporations, PACs,

Super PACs, and 501 (C)(4) tax-exempt groups advocate for policy in Washington, politicians will be accountable to them...not the American people. If the NRA can direct millions of dollars into a campaign and concentrate advertising to siphon support from other candidates, they hold the cards. Money in politics, especially after the landmark Citizens United v. Federal Election Commission decision in January 2010, will only pull the power away from the people (everyday Americans) and hand it off to corporations and advocacy groups. (The Citizens United decision protects independent political expenditures under the guise of Free Speech.) So if we really want to regain control of our political representation, we need to demand Citizens United be overturned.

When the lawyers of presidential candidates draft nondisclosure agreements (NDAs) buying the silence of women, there is a problem with the system. The potential for a personal bombshell, like an extramarital affair, is not new to politics...but it shouldn't be part of the ball game at all. Hush money is a violation of campaign finance laws and should be seen as a political foul ball. If it's clear that the funds were used to silence someone who's voice might have influenced the election, that's a strike. If they tried to hide the transaction from the public, that's another strike, and if the investigation into the cover-up is interfered with...that's three strikes, you're out.

Making Elections More Practical

Elections in America are far more difficult than they need to be. We make the process confusing and involvement by the general public problematic. (This is especially true amongst urban, liberal voters.) Elections are a time consuming, news-overbearing, tiring process that cost billions of dollars. Many Americans wish to have a voice in the political discourse, especially at the local level, but are shut out by family commitments and conflicts with their employment. It's hard to get to the ballot box on a weekday when you're balancing work and providing for your family. The process is even harder if you can't understand the lingo, how to vote, or what you're voting for.

Demanding a shorter campaign period should also be a top priority. Today's election seasons, especially in presidential contests, begin immediately after the general election polls close. Politicians seeking reelection are always running, causing their focus to be centered on retaining their seats instead of actually governing. By following the lead of Canada, where election seasons only last ten and a half weeks, we could limit the amount of news each campaign cycle consumes. Since our population is larger and more widely spread out, we'll no doubt need more than three months, but certainly we can nominate candidates, hold debates, and make a selection in less than 4 years (2 years for Congressional Representatives). Scaling back the ever-increasing duration of our elections should be a top priority. While we're at it, we need to tweak the voting period to increase early voting. Given the chance to cast their ballots early, more Americans will be able to participate in the revered role of electing their representation.

Elections could take place on weekends, when most Americans have the day off. Today our elections occur on Tuesdays simply because in the 1800's farmers in agrarian America needed at least a day to travel by horse to the ballot box. (Market day for crop sales was Wednesday; Sunday was the Biblical Sabbath) With the convenience of holding elections on a Tuesday no longer relevant, it's time for a change. While today's polling places are more prevalent and many voters are able to make their mark just miles from their homes, our elections system has become a great expense.

If changing the date of the election is just too radical, perhaps making Election Day an official U.S. holiday will bring out more voters. Though there will always be people forced to work on Election Day, putting it on a holiday could bring in voters who otherwise might not make it to the polls. Unfortunately, this would only further increase the already overwhelming cost of our electoral processes. In any event, we could elongate the voting window, allowing extra days so voters who work on one day (say Sunday) could vote on another (say Friday). This too would increase the cost, but perhaps widening the election period would allow more voters to cast their ballots.

America would be best served, however, by following the lead of the Beaver State. Oregon has used a vote-by-mail system since 1998 and increased its percentage of recorded voters after passing a law that automatically registers citizens when they apply for a driver's license or identification card at the DMV. For the price of a Forever Stamp, voters across America could make their voices heard, utilizing a system that studies show is more secure and fair than in-person voting. It's secure because each paper ballot can be recounted, unlike digital polling utilized in some states that leaves no paper trail. Those digital polls are also more susceptible to hacking, voter fraud, and machine tampering. If postage were paid, there would be no reason not to vote. Several Western states use a form of mail-in-ballot system; the process saves these states significant voting expenses. If we must continue with in-person voting, let's make it fair and secure, ensuring we don't suppress anyone's voice. Given the obvious Russian intervention in the 2016 election and their willingness to do it again, it would be best if we had a paper trail for every vote to prevent another compromised election.

A motor-voter system (like Oregon's) would prevent Americans from being turned away from the ballot box each year for trivial issues. No one should be excluded because they lack an identity document or are impeded by a physical or mental disability. Under a motor voter registration process, every American citizen would already be registered and receive their ballot in the mail, removing any question about their legal right to vote. There would be no reason to require a valid state identification card, driver's license, or U.S passport to prove a voter's identity. Not everyone living in states that employ conventional voting methods has an unexpired document, even if they are legally qualified to vote. In those states, ill-informed polling staff, who believe that fraud is being attempted when two individuals present IDs with the same first and last name, often turn away minority communities from the voting booth. Consistently, these similarities are just coincidence. Many cultures have common names like John Smith, Maria Hernandez, or Mohamed Kahn. In fact, according to the U.S. Elections Project, only 35 out of over 834 million votes cast between 2000 and 2014 were considered "credible" allegations of voter impersonation. Unfortunately, ignorance and personal prejudice can block an American's constitutional obligation to elect their political representatives. Therefore, migrating to a motor-voter system would prevent this type of voter suppression.

Unseating the Political Class

We also have an obligation to make politics more available to the general public. The founding fathers never envisioned America would be run by a political class, but rather by common people, giving of their time in service to their country. We need to overhaul our political system to make it easier for everyday Americans, not just the affluent or politically immersed, to be a part of the discussion.

Every American has a unique voice to offer, but as long as incumbent politicians hold a monopoly on their seats, we'll never hear what average Americans have to say. Even from our country's inception, George Washington knew it was important to step down after two terms as president to set an example that our politicians are not kings. Unfortunately, today many Senators and Representatives hold their seats for decades. Governors and mayors often return to office after brief hiatuses to circumvent term limits. As long as the same (primarily older) men and women call the shots, we'll keep making the same mistakes. Many politicians who hold the same seat in a chamber of Congress for decades are beholden to special interests and lobbyists who continue to bankroll their reelection efforts. Our representation needs a fresh, youthful boost of energy just as NFL, NBA, NHL, and MLB teams need a refresh of players every now and then. (Who'd have a better chance of winning a game as quarterback, an 80-year-old or a 30-year-old?)

Making Elections Understandable

In addition to these key provisions, we need to work on making electoral methods more understandable to the masses. Few people can artfully explain in layman's terms how a proportional representation system can give a candidate that loses the popular vote more delegates, or why a caucus is less suitable than a primary, or even why competing in California is different than running in New Hampshire where candidates employ "retail politics". Delegate selection rules need to be addressed by both parties, including the use of unpledged delegates. By doing a better job defining primary guidelines, Republicans and Democrats would allow for greater participation of more informed voters. Primary election reform would not only increase voter involvement, but also increase political debate across the country. Having more back and forth exchanges with Americans of all stripes would, in turn, increase our probability of creating change. Additionally, these simple reforms would make the system more balanced, giving even first-time candidates a shot at winning, without needing a vast legal team to navigate confusing procedures.

Combatting Election Tampering

Democracy only exists if we protect it, and one key aspect of any democratic institution is the legitimacy of an election. Unlike other countries that put on sham demonstrations while pretending to be a democracy, America has always been committed to impartial, unprejudiced, and clean elections. When our electoral processes are undermined and foreign powers position their own minion in our seat of power, the foundation of our democracy is called into question.

Presidential procrastination and Congressional dithering over the clear interference in America's 2016 election is self-sabotage. After the mesmerizing results on Election Day, we are slowly piecing together what happened, but we're not preparing for the worst. We know now that our elections weren't just tampered with, but weaponized against the interests of the American people. The elements behind the outright theft of our election in 2016, the Russians, will be back next time around. The perpetrators will reuse the same tactics they know will work and employ new means for circumventing our limited firewalls. They'll once again target counties/states with outdated election hardware and software, likely getting even further now that they've had time to better analyze how our systems work. While we continue to measure the scope of their influence in the 2016 election – possibly branching out to include the prior primaries and down-ballot races – they'll come at us again. If we don't actively work to shut down their interference, they'll get away with it once more, slowly whittling our democracy down to its core.

The United States has a long history of demanding free and fair elections in democracies around the globe. As a significant nation builder in the 20th Century, we've set up, inspected, and managed voter registration, ballot boxes, and entire elections. With the intent of chaperoning democracy in every corner of the globe, America has called for international oversight when dictatorial regimes conduct "show elections" instead of authentic referendums of choice. We've called out rubber-stamp elections, monitored attempts to delegitimize electoral victories, and educated voters to recognize coercion and vote rigging. Why wouldn't we call for the same oversight here at home?

States and even the country as a whole cannot be expected to operate without supervision. Congress has the immediate tutelage under the law to validate the election, however their approval is generally a thumbs-up rather than a detailed examination. After each victory in the Electoral College, a joint session of Congress is convened to certify the decision of the electors. That's the first line of defense. However, the possibility for even Congressional leaders to kowtow to the malevolent actors behind a rigged election demands that we have additional mechanisms available to verify the legitimacy of a victory and the impartiality of the election that decided it. Here again is the need for a third party group, a multilateral organization or supranational institution to oversee the campaigns before and the results after the election.

Just as some third world countries have used our watchful eye to monitor their ballot casting process, we could lean on the Swiss, the French, the Brits, or even the Aussies to give us an impartial review. Mandatory secondary recounts and paper printouts for every vote would also cement the legitimacy of any win or find the culprit of any meddling.

The process of creating an election monitoring process isn't easy. Such a political leviathan of legal oversight would almost certainly need to be organized under a constitutional amendment, ratified by the states. Unfortunately, the current sentiment of the Supreme Court precludes the addition of any further amendments beyond the current 27 with the Justices seeing the constitutionality of a change to the supreme law of the land as an undesirable catch-22. Even if the Judicial Branch would allow it, legislative decisions that have wide appeal, like the Equal Rights Act, have been unable to make the cut. Most importantly, there is an evident absence of bipartisan consensus across the country for such reforms, making it almost impossible to garner a victory in the ratification process. Considering that Republicans (seemingly the biggest detractors) monopolize most state legislative bodies, it's not likely to be in the cards until we shuffle the deck.

While we deliberate how best to monitor our elections for future meddling, we must actively work to intercept new efforts to attack our elections. If such a constitutional amendment were initiated today, based on historical comparison, it may take several hundred years to ratify – having required just 202 years for the 27th Amendment, while even more continue to remain un-ratified. In the meantime, we need to defensively protect our elections by investing in a total overhaul of our dated ballot casting systems. We certainly have the technology, the know-how (computer wizards), and the financial capability to thwart any invasion by a foreign power, known adversary, or political organization. The real question is whether we have the willpower to act and for that, the answer is no.

A majority of American politicians in Washington DC don't seem to care that our elections were meddled in. More than a year later, we've done nothing to take corrective action or prevent a repeat of 2016. Why? It starts at the top. If the highest echelons of American leadership are comfortable with the status quo, nothing will change. Regardless of his participation or advance knowledge, the Russian meddling in 2016 benefitted Donald Trump. Therefore he stands, not to gain, but to lose by promoting any efforts to secure our voter registration and ballot casting systems. In fact, he has taken offense to suggestions that our onetime inviolable electoral process was subverted by the Russians so as to guarantee his victory against Secretary Clinton.

Instead of shying away from the culprits, America needs to fix the problem and punish the perpetrators. When a burglar breaks into your home, you fix the weakness at their point of entry and make sure they serve time for their assault on your security. If they get in, steal something, and get out without your knowledge, you still fix the problem and then track down the bad guy and make him pay. In the case of election meddling, that punishment will vary based on the severity of the intrusion. If an entity breaks in, looks around and doesn't change anything, the punishment should be limited to economic sanctions and admonishment within the international community. If data is changed and alters the "free and fair" aspect of an election by influencing a different result than what otherwise would have occurred, the response should be significantly abrasive. Each administration has its own national security strategy that details the specifics of a proportional response. Depending on the hawkish nature of the man (or woman) who devised the policy and the president behind the desk, that plan of action could include any number of economic, political, or military responses. We must be prepared to take the necessary action and accept the potential consequences of a damaging strike. But if we fail to act because we're scared, our democracy will eventually flounder. In the case of 2016, that seems to be the path Congressional Republicans are okay following – they prefer not to even discuss solutions or reprimands.

By doing nothing, Republicans and the conservative Democrats who often caucus with the political right, are sanctioning continued foreign meddling. To date, America hasn't done anything at all to prevent future attacks on our elections and that apathy stems from President Trump. If he accepts (and he won't or at least not in emphatic terms) that Russia helped elect him, he is calling the legitimacy of his election into question. In order to protect his ego, Trump will never recognize the pervasive hacking of America's elections, electrical grid, and financial supercomputers. Sadly the lethargy to take corrective action is cyclical too. By not doing anything, we allow it to happen again. Mark Twain once offered this astute advice for preventing the echoes of misfortune and failure, "history doesn't repeat itself, but it often rhymes". If we once again elect a leader hand-picked by a foreign power, they too won't do anything either so as to protect their political prowess and appearance of legitimacy.

End Gerrymandering

Every American should examine the shape of their home district. Does it have straight lines and form a natural shape that matches the contours of state lines? Suspiciously, no single district in the country makes sense unless you are a political party who has manipulated it to your benefit. That is simply not fair...simply un-America. Our congressional districts should evenly reflect the number of people in them, not reflect a partisan agenda by carving out alcoves of red in liberal states and limiting blue districts to major cities.

We need to focus on how to even the odds by diminishing the stranglehold the GOP has on the House of Representatives. Through strategic gerrymandering, Republicans have gradually made Congress increasingly lopsided for decades. While our country is divided politically, Republicans appear to be in the majority because of their dominance in the U.S. Congress and in state legislatures. That advantage is surreptitious, however, as only 22 percent of the country identifies as Republican. A further 32 percent are affiliated with the Democratic Party and 44 percent lie somewhere in between (politically independent). Unbeknownst to most Americans, the GOP has constructed a winning strategy to deter election fairness and augment conservative victories nationwide. Through state house and gubernatorial victories, Republicans have built a rigid backbone to counter the fewer states controlled by the Democratic Party, allowing them to rewrite district lines. Doing so, they increase the conservative margin in Congress, shore up victories on policy, and grow closer to their goal of instigating an Article Five Convention or Federal Convention where the U.S. Constitution could be amended by a 2/3rds majority of state legislatures.

With an Amendments Convention (as the Article Five process is also called) the GOP would have the ability to rewrite the Constitution to match their party platform, doing away with hard-fought freedoms for women like Roe v. Wade, for the LGBTQ community like Obergefell v. Hodges, and perhaps even strengthening the 2nd Amendment to reduce regulation on firearms or required background checks. This is in direct discord with what our forefathers envisioned. The framers of the Constitution created the provision with the hopes of preventing the federal government from running unchecked. They deliberately gave power to the people through their Congressional representatives and elected executives so as not to create coalitions aimed at passing partisan political agendas. Such an obsequious plot to undermine the foundations of government by convening an Article Five Convention is not just a possibility, but is in fact, a core objective of the current Republican Party.

It is imperative that Democrats, Independents, Libertarians, Greens, and nonpartisans prevent the Grand Ole Party from driving the country singlehandedly. Ours was meant to be a nation with divided ideologies, switching majorities between parties to slowly move the country forward. That's why gerrymandering reform should be signature to the liberal platform moving forward. Democrats and Independents must pledge to make a real effort of ensuring district mapping is fairly decided. Former President Obama has vowed to make gerrymandering reversal a primary aspiration of his work post-presidency, a task he is already undertaking with his former Attorney General Eric Holder. However, a former president, presidential foundation, and a former Attorney General can't fix conservative gerrymandering. It will take victories in red districts; in red, blue, and purple states; and a concentrated effort to prevail in every race from statewide office to the White House.

When people say Congress isn't working, they're right...it isn't working, because it doesn't fairly represent the people like it's supposed to under Article One of the U.S. Constitution. We have the power to redraw districts to better match the people within the state, in a nonpartisan and fair way, that doesn't benefit any one party. Doing so would create a Congress whose representatives would be held accountable to the people of the state they serve. Such a revision would guarantee Congress works – it would once again represent the American people, not a political party.

In a redrawn America, some states would be solid red whereas others would gain enough blue districts to look like a checkerboard. With a fair redistricting, Democrats would gain a majority of Congressional seats, which would more accurately represent the liberal leaning of the country. Windows for redistricting are small, generally occurring immediately after a national census every 10 years. In most states, the state legislature (twenty-eight directly and a few indirectly) is given the responsibility to redistrict, although governors generally have oversight and input in that process. With the exception of the seven states with just one congressional representative (Alaska, Delaware, Montana, North Dakota, South Dakota, Vermont, and Wyoming) even districting is central to a fair representation in Congress.

Leave No Race Uncontested

Many states have historically been less favorable of liberal politics and are written off by the Democratic Party as "too red to flip". Likely Democrats will never win in these districts, states, and sub-sects of the country, but that should not stop them from trying. Every election cycle, Democrats miss out on opportunities to win and spread their agenda because races are left uncontested. They need to run everywhere they can and run on the policies they stand for, backing strong candidates who can win in the red zones.

Democrats need to refresh their tactics and go beyond the Howard Dean approach. A new Fifty State Strategy can focus on winning state races, governorships, Congressional districts, Senate contests, and the White House. There are no "unwinnable" states, territories, or commonwealths in our union where Democrats cannot be competitive. They won't win every state or in every election year and they likely won't win some states ever, but Democrats should stay focused on a larger map. Allocating resources, running good candidates, and making every effort will allow Democrats to have a chance at bringing change to all locales, especially those that need it most.

A Fifty State Strategy is often misunderstood by the general public as a political approach to winning 50 states in the Electoral College during a presidential election. Yet the better strategy wouldn't focus on trying to win each state in a presidential election year. Instead, it would incorporate the statewide, district, and local races, along with U.S. House and Senate contests, in an attempt to give one party a majority or supermajority across the country. (Essentially, a Fifty State Strategy should be focused on long-term competitiveness instead of individual electoral victories.) That's exactly what Republicans have been doing at the state level, allowing them to unfairly redistrict states to increase their margin in Congress. A wider ground-game – designed to make every race contestable, locate strong candidates, and develop fundraising mechanisms – is an absolute must if Democrats want to see change.

Repair the Damage of 2016

Democrats aren't the only ones who need a new strategy. The Trump –Make America Great Again – smoke and mirrors campaign won't work next time around. Hopefully, Republicans will recognize they were duped by Trump and Russian meddling efforts in 2016 and will be prepared to never allow it to happen again. With any luck, they won't accept another unqualified candidate or an unconstructed agenda that weighs down their efforts to promote their conservative values. Instead of grading future nominees on the Trump Curve, where anything goes, Republicans will have to closely examine each candidate's experience, ideas, behavior, and background, so as not to once again embarrass the party.

The Republican Party will have to restore its integrity. After backing a leader that insults, bullies, lies, and shifts blame, the Grand Ole Party's image has been tarnished. The public's impression of a Bully-in-Chief, surrounded by meek party legislators kowtowing to the whims of a wannabe autocrat, has laid ruin to a once reputable party of conservative statesmen. Reporters catch Republican Senators and Congressmen ducking into bathrooms, running through obscure basement hallways, and blockading themselves in their offices so that they won't have to face the questions and ire of their constituents. Some don't even go home to their states or clear "full mailboxes" on their phone answering machines in fear that they will be verbally accosted by the very people that they are supposed to represent. Too many are owned by the NRA and other big lobbyists, or simply fear that if they oppose the President he will negatively tweet about them and hurt their chances come time for reelection. Conservatives will have to find strong, honest, reputable leaders (unburdened by personal or political scandal) to restock their stable of candidates.

Republicans need to return to the uniting values that our country was once known for – the basic bargain of doing good for all and collectively bettering ourselves. Our forefathers knew that the government they were organizing would have to progress to keep up with the changing times. They tried to implement a form of government with checks and balances that would mature with the country's needs and to prevent any one group or person from being all-powerful. They sought a united country of people who seek certain basic freedoms to work together and look to the future. Along with Democrats and Independents, Republicans can lead the charge in putting America back on the right track.

Conservatives have many clear goals, ones that they share with Independents, unaffiliated voters, and a few Democrats. From infrastructure investment to a strong sense of national security, Republican ideas are an important part of our country's political dialogue. Few major legislative victories have come from one party and no good policy has ever been achieved through strictly partisan practices. That importance of bipartisanship is the crucial point of contention that the Grand Ole Party must take action on. Will the GOP continue to block out the bright light of change – their view obstructed by partisan blinders – or will they acknowledge that via bilateral cooperation we can together foster a brighter future for America? The choice is not up to party kingpins or conservative representatives in Washington; it's up to their bosses, the right-leaning electorate that supplies them with the votes they need to remain in power.

Both sides of the aisle are going to have to take Russia's targeted influence campaign seriously. The gravity of foreign intervention in our elections (a clear component of the 2016 electoral result) should unify our country, not divide it. We should all be concentrated on thwarting such an intolerable manipulation of our democratic electoral activities. We need to also focus on punishing the Russian Federation to dissuade future attacks targeting more susceptible democracies around the globe. Even as Democrats and Republicans must work across party lines on the Russian election interference question, it shouldn't take a stolen election to bring the two sides together. Whatever happened to the words – negotiate, compromise, togetherness? Bipartisan cooperation should be the bedrock of our Legislative Branch, just as our Executive Branch should be focused on implementing a nonpartisan plan of action that benefits all Americans...not just one political party.

Revolutionizing Social Media

If we don't address our errors in 2016, we'll keep making the same mistakes. One of those errors was the dissemination of materials on social media to support Trump...and it worked. The Donald is also the reason why we can't get any traction on reform. He is protecting himself by refusing to move the conversation forward. If we can't even talk about what happened, we can't start fixing it. So far we've done nothing because we can't seem to get past the politics. Issues like the Internet (appropriate/non-expletive content) and social media shouldn't need to be regulated, but they do. They shouldn't be political either, but they are.

In 2016, social media was used against us as Russia turned our affinity for impersonal communication into a tool for propaganda distribution. They broadcast fake news stories, created phony profiles, shared bogus rumors, and recruited millions of unknowing accomplices in their mission to elect Donald Trump. They used the unregulated social media platforms many Americans still look to every day for news and current events to impart a narrative that boosted Trump's persona and tore down Clinton's esteem. We should have done something years ago to make social media safer from circulating fake news and less of a target to foreign propaganda, but we didn't. Now it'll be even harder to do, but we must start the process or the problem will continue. Next time, who knows which party will be the target?

The biggest hurdle is regulation. At the time of the 2016 election, there were no safeguards in place to prevent individual users or Russian espionage organizations from creating hundreds of sham accounts or replicating Trump supporters, news agencies, and trustworthy sources of information. The void of guidelines allowing this manipulation of the American people is a direct result of Congressional failure to stay current or demand a watchdog of sorts until social media regulation could be enacted.

Corporations cannot self-regulate, they just can't be trusted to do it on their own. It is entirely impossible to run a for-profit corporation while policing yourself, especially when deregulation is more lucrative to the company's bottom line. Simply, social media platforms like Facebook and Twitter make more money when they don't enforce tight restrictions. Once they begin changing their process, revenues will fall through the floor. Congress could and likely will impose new laws that require social media sites to comb through posts, pages, and profiles to eliminate fake users, but that process will take years. Billions of Facebook users and some 325+ million Twitter profiles will take time to verify. In the meantime, new fake accounts will be created and more misinformation posts will be shared.

Even if all the social media bots, Twitter eggs (users who hide their identity behind the indistinctive default image of anonymity), and fake news Facebook pages are deleted, real users will still spread/share content. If their sources off social media platforms and from other pages on the Internet are bogus, so too will be the posts they share. What is posted on the Internet is hardly ever supported by multiple sources, unless the content originates from a respected media outlet. Even still, inaccurate and politically distorted materials can be hidden in the subtext. As a nation, we've become numb to the inaccuracy of what is shared widely on social media and perhaps have been unknowingly disseminating propaganda that benefits interests other than our own. In 2016, rumors that Hillary Clinton was running a child sex ring in a DC pizza shop or supplying arms to terror groups were shared widely across social media. Most users knew they were falsehoods meant to change minds, but some unknowingly re-tweeted or shared the content to their followers – continuing the cycle.

Technically, Facebook and Twitter already do monitor posts for specific content, but there are noticeable gaps. Both employ AI (Artificial Intelligence) to monitor posts for hate speech, which itself is poorly defined and rarely obvious. They don't currently scrutinize individual posts, line for line, to determine the validity of the arguments made or the appearance of propaganda content to imitate actual news. They do provide user controls, allowing each page owner to decide what content they see or to hide content that they deem is irrelevant. Users can also flag inappropriate posts or ask Facebook/Twitter to review materials on the company's site, plus they can determine what type of advertisements they will see based on the content they post or subscribe to. Facebook and Twitter do verify celebrity, commercial, and authentic accounts of public interest, but to unsuspecting users, replica accounts may appear genuine. In other words, someone could create a page that looks like it belongs to Donald Trump's campaign, share information declaring it is official campaign content, and make people think the page is connected to the campaign, when really it is run by a Russian named Yuri who works for the Kremlin. Adding to the problem, there is nothing preventing users from maintaining multiple pages, allowing groups like the Internet Research Agency to run hundreds of propaganda ads across tens of thousands of unique pages.

Unfortunately for us, the problem with fake news dissemination is the First Amendment protection of free speech. Under the standard interpretation of the Constitution, even inaccurate or leading commentary (fake news/alternative facts) is considered "free speech". That is to say, you can share something patently false, defamatory or not, and the only recourse one could take is a personal lawsuit (libel/slander) if they thought the post diminished their public image or damaged them somehow. Even as the FBI has investigated individuals for sharing "fake news", there is no statute allowing them to demand that information be taken down or corrected. There simply are no chaperones putting masking tape on the door, making sure everyone is staying in the right room. Instead, the Internet is a free-for-all and while independent watchdog groups monitor and patrol the alternative facts swirling around the web, only a few repulsively illegal activities are regulated.

America started the Internet as a means of communicating with our missile silos. We made it public in the 1990s during the Clinton administration and it quickly spread around the globe, out of control. The intent was to bring people together and support global commerce, not promote propaganda or explicit materials. If we started it, we should be able to regulate it. Unfortunately, it's just a little too late. If we regulate the Internet, we can only control web traffic within or that crosses through the United States. We can't tell an Italian ISP what services they can offer or regulate the website of Spanish clothing company ZARA. We can put limitations/boundaries on the version of those sites visible to Americans. We can make those sites unavailable to Americans...but then we'll be accused of pulling a North Korea. Communist China, the DPRK, and Russia (really any nondemocratic country) censor their Internet to prevent access to information that could undermine the power-grasp of their leadership. Long story short – too late – we need to control pages like Facebook and Twitter that don't belong to who they say they do but not go so far as to infringe on free speech.

Divert From Party Line Voting

Politics is deeply tribal (especially at the state and local level), with most voting according to the party affiliation of the candidate not their experience, position on issues, or character. I don't personally care for the duopoly of our two-party system as most people today have a very black and white view on political issues, voting party lines because of what matters most to them. (Or more often than not, because of the R or D symbol next to a name.) Many voters will cast their votes straight down the party line, without listening to what political candidates say or taking the time to research different issues. Some who were raised in a family that was Republican or Democrat vote the same way as their parents or grandparents. I grant that many also vote the opposite way, not because they believe differently so much as they want to separate themselves from their family's viewpoints.

One year I was in Iowa and Nebraska before an election and talked to voters who said they would always cast their ballot for the Republican or always vote for the Democrat...no matter what. Their ethos was locked on to voting one way or the other, regardless of the candidate, issues, or policy. Instead of party-line voting,

Americans should select their candidates by the issues they support, their history, experience, behavior, and values. We should be able to vote for what we believe, not just for the candidate of our political party. We should feel good about ourselves when we differ with our party base and support the policy of a candidate that is more in line with our own beliefs and values. While I have campaigned for, donated to, and worked with Democratic candidates (from state representatives to presidential candidates), I have to live by my values and my integrity. I can't always support a candidate just because their party affiliation matches mine. This is especially true of politicians who switch party membership with the hopes of single-handedly moving the party's platform in a specific direction, or because they faced stiff competition in a primary. They should vote their conscience, vote for what they believe is best, and refrain from pretending they're something they're not. If a Democratic politician in a red state cares more about reelection (capitulating to the Republican agenda) than the fundamentals of the Democratic platform, they should change their affiliation or drop out. We simply don't have the luxury of do-overs in politics and by only supporting a party when their seat in Congress isn't on the line, politicians jeopardize the potential for real change. While party platforms evolve often, generally incorporating new ideas every four years, the party affiliation isn't mandatory. If a Congressional leader or presidential candidate is really an Independent or non-partisan, they should run that way. A third viewpoint is better than a last-minute stab in the back when they vote against their own party on an important piece of legislation that their constituents were counting on them to support, defend, or reject.

In 2016, many Republicans parted from the Trump campaign,

recognizing he didn't stand for traditional conservative principles or espouse the values they wanted to see in a president. They did it again in 2017, voting for the Democrat (Doug Jones) in Alabama's Special U.S. Senate Election – also making a stand regarding the questionable ethics and history of the GOP candidate. One should never vote for a candidate or ballot measure because of party affiliation. Instead, we should vote for what's best for our community, state, and country.

Clear Messaging and Strong Party Backing

Democrats can compete nationwide when they share their message and connect with voters. They're not a party of leftist or socialist liberals, hell-bent on reforming every aspect of government, nor are they Marxist-communists seeking to destroy the democratic foundations our country was founded on. Democrats are a party about people, children and families, the disenfranchised, and a party focused on changing America's future for the better. Conceding congressional districts, states, or whole sections of the country to conservatives only allows the Republican Party to bolster their strength, blocking Democratic chances to flip those regions later.

In the aftermath of the historic 2016 loss, Democrats need to aim high, go for broke, and put strong candidates on the ballot in every race across the country – every single cycle. They can't be limited to focusing on the races they know they can win. Democrats need a new approach, one that goes beyond Stronger Together or Change We Can Believe In. They need a new strategy to win for their party, their values, and their country. While it seems like an uphill battle (and it undoubtedly is), it's not impossible and it shouldn't be written off by not trying. When a blue candidate competes in a red district, they need every tool available to them to reach out to voters, connect with people on substance, and make a dent in the partisan divides that keep a district liberal or conservative. As a party, Democrats need to outline a clear blueprint for a successful effort to win on the merits of progressive values, the content of a candidate's character, and the importance of the issues the party continues to champion.

I grew up in Southwestern Oregon, spending much of my youth in the rural state. My county (Curry County) had been struggling economically many years before my family built our home there in the early 1990s. The timber and fishing industry, along with the area's notorious lily bulb farming, had been on the decline for years. As a result, the county was uncompetitive with the rest of the state, especially the populated Willamette Valley cities of Eugene, Corvallis, Salem, and Portland. As a small, struggling, rural area predominantly populated by people on fixed incomes, Curry County has been dominated by conservative politics for decades, most voters being lifelong card-carrying Republicans and passionate NRA supporters.

In the year after I graduated from college, I was asked to consider running for the State Senate or State House seat representing Curry County. I love Southern Oregon, but I was not at all interested in living there for the rest of my life. Intrigued by the opportunity but not seriously interested in running yet for an elected office, I met with local Democratic Party leaders to discuss a potential campaign. They were thrilled that a young man was interested and considering a run against the timeworn Republicans that served in Oregon's 1st House/Senate District seats. The local party leadership was hopeful that due to the scandals challenging the two elected representatives, a new face could win in November.

Ultimately I declined to run, leaving them with a few of my strategic ideas for how to be successful and offering to assist them with campaign tactics. Unfortunately, the local party ended up supporting two older gentlemen (both highly respected by their friends and neighbors) to run for the two seats. Both lost by wide margins in an election year where Democrats in the rest of the state took conclusive victories and increased the party's majority in the State House, Senate, and statewide offices. The Democrats came up short because their candidates were lacking passion, energy, party support, or a clear message. Both men had little political campaign experience, and neither had a large following or public presence in which to gain support. On Election Day, the only thing most people knew about them was their party affiliation – thanks to the capital D next to their name on the ballot. Neither had taken widespread opportunity to spell out their plans, share their beliefs, or connect with their potential constituency. Most importantly, they lacked the resources from the Democratic Party necessary to differentiate themselves from the incumbents who were under scrutiny for questionable unethical behavior and outrageous public remarks. I don't blame either candidate for the loss, I blame the system that worked against the Democrats in rural Oregon, in red districts and states across the country, and anywhere that the party had conceded was "unwinnable".

Move Forward

After the 2016 General Election, the Democratic Party was weakened. They were forced into the minority in both chambers of Congress, lost the White House, had a slim chance of maintaining a center-left Supreme Court, and were well behind Republicans in state legislature and gubernatorial control. In order to reclaim the America we all want to see, we need a more balanced government, one that represents the diverse view of the country, Americans of all backgrounds. (That balance includes both conservatives and liberals.) The Democratic Party has a long way to go to win back majorities in state houses, Congress, and the White House, but it's not an impossible climb towards a strong liberal majority in American politics once again.

We can start moving forward by changing the way we operate. While it's important for Democrats to be successful, compete in every race, and win on the national stage, it's crucial that liberals also work with the political right to find cross-party solutions to our collective problems. Nothing will be solved by one voice, one perspective, or one idea. The American Experiment will fail if we move away from us/we and towards I/me. An "I alone can fix it" strategy will always be doomed by the weakness of the individual, but when we all come together – starting today – and lend our distinct voices and unique talents, there's nothing we can't cooperatively accomplish tomorrow.

CHAPTER SIXTEEN: TOMORROW

Tomorrow, and tomorrow, and tomorrow,
Creeps in this petty pace from day to day,
To the last syllable of recorded time;
And all our yesterdays have lighted fools
The way to dusty death. Out, out, brief candle!
Life's but a walking shadow, a poor player,
That struts and frets his hour upon the stage,
And then is heard no more. It is a tale
Told by an idiot, full of sound and fury,
Signifying nothing.
-Quote from the William Shakespeare tragedy *Macbeth*

As a senior in high school, I was begrudgingly tasked with memorizing and reciting a stanza from Shakespeare's *Macbeth*, a verse that would be shared in front of the class. At the time I didn't fully understand the purpose of the lesson, requiring sleep-deprived students to reiterate a seemingly meaningless stave from a tragedy written centuries before. The task was made especially tedious since *Macbeth* was composed in the unfamiliar Old English text. The practice of memorization has helped me in numerous ways, especially when I was on the stump sharing my story with people in Iowa, California, and Washington during the election season. However, it wasn't until the dramatic climax of the 2016 electoral cycle and the first days of the Trump Administration that I realized the significance of that almost poetic canto I had committed to memory years earlier.

The Tomorrow Soliloquy delivered by Macbeth, in the tragedy of the same name, comes as the protagonist of the story realizes his fate is upon him. As his enemy McDuff besieges the castle, Macbeth maintains confidence in his ability to thwart the impending attack. In the distance, a woman cries out in fear…a sound that once would have startled perhaps even scared Macbeth, but has little effect on him. He's heard and seen far worse; now nothing can surprise him, nothing can shock him. Macbeth later learns that shriek was his wife, screaming in terror at her death. Macbeth is killed by the man he had used to gain power (MacDuff), blaming his predecessor's death on MacDuff to absolve himself of the murder.

While the tale of Macbeth may not seem anything like the politics of America in the 21st Century, there are lessons to be learned from the 17th Century anecdote. To me, the Tomorrow speech is an allegory about politics in general. When we are so focused on our yesterdays, our failures and our disagreements, we neglect to look to the future and what tomorrow can bring. Today is too late to think about yesterday! It's the time to think about tomorrow and what we can do to make our country better, safer, and more inclusive. We have to look forward and dream big. We have to break down barriers and aim for the stars. Only then can we start to make progress, only then can we make America greater.

The Shakespearian analogy also tenders some advice for the more underhanded Machiavellian types who try to surreptitiously sabotage our democratic elections. The poetic justice at the end of the well-known tragedy, Macbeth's death at the hands of the man he framed for murder (MacDuff), cements the avowal that in the end, good always beats evil. Similarly, it offers a potential roadmap for how deception, fraud, and mendacious activities will ultimately betray the guilty party. If you spread falsities, make poor decisions and exploit someone else to obtain power, the result is almost certainly failure. Whereas if you earn the support of your people legitimately, you'll not only feel better about yourself, but will likely stay in power longer.

"Life's but a walking shadow" – a few moments in the spotlight and decades in obscurity. We can't let our leaders take us out of the fight for freedom, for human rights, or for global peace and prosperity because they're afraid of failure. If we want to be the "shining city upon a hill" that President Reagan envisioned, we must break out of the darkness and lead the world from the foreground. We have to be bold, take risks, and own our mistakes.

We can be the light of the world, a beacon of hope in the darkness, if we return to our values and challenge others to follow our lead. Instead of getting distracted by our political differences, let's work together to solve the real problems holding Americans back. We must endeavor to work with our allies and enemies alike building a better world for everyone and guaranteeing the most basic human rights for all. Let us encourage other countries to find within them their better angels and to provide for their people the freedoms and liberties America has championed since our invention of modern democracy.

America has always been a place where inspiration and innovation take precedence over division and obstruction. A place where light could expel darkness, and love could trump hate (pun intended). As a global power, we have an obligation to spread love and kindness, to promote justice, and oppose inequality. We have a role in crafting a better future for our planet by leading the fight for clean energy and being the prominent voice in reducing carbon emissions. We have a responsibility to stand-up for the voiceless, here at home and around the globe, to advocate for inclusivity of all.

The world is watching. They have been keeping an eye on us every day since we took the reins in the early 20th Century as a global power and the title "Leader of the Free World". Many countries have crafted their democracy in our fashion; others are molding a new frontier based on our example. We inspire hope to those struggling under oppressive governments and provide an illustration of a freer, fairer world to those who are constricted by human rights atrocities. We stimulate opportunity in every corner of the map, along every latitude of the globe, and in every country on Earth.

America can't sit on the sidelines, we can't stay in the darkness, and we can't hide in the shadows. We have to lead and set the example for the rest of the world. We have to run fast, aim high, and fight hard to overcome the challenges we face and make the world a better place for everyone. It's up to all of us to be the change we want to see, here in America and around the world. We owe it to our founding fathers to continue to grow the American Experiment they crafted so many years ago.

Tomorrow will undoubtedly bring new challenges, but hopefully it will also include a few opportunities to learn, grow, and make a difference. So let us not give up! Let us not lose hope.

Make America Stronger Together Again

We must remain focused on the future, honed in on a vision of togetherness and inclusivity. Most importantly, let's commit ourselves to never stop fighting for a better America – one that generates prosperity through collective action. For too long it's been us versus them, but we can't have that attitude anymore. We must work together to solve the problems we face, reaching across party lines to find common ground. The challenges of the future will be greater than ever, requiring even more from us. We shouldn't let our divisions blockade America from being the best we can be.

Since that unique and gloomy Election Night on November 8th, 2016, we've grown even further apart than ever before. The challenges we face as a nation are too big to be tackled unilaterally. We can only address the big-ticket issues if we come together and find a way to work with our adversaries. We must unite as a country and get past the divisions that threaten to rip us apart. We can't expect to accomplish anything if we continue to pit ourselves against our friends and neighbors, allowing trivial quarrels or differences in opinion to come between us.

This is not just a political problem. We have to solve our divisions at home just as we do in Washington. We must accept our neighbors and look beyond how they voted in 2016 or any other election. When politicians of both parties suggest we have "more that unites us than divides us", they're right. It's not just a talking point or platitude. We've always shared confidence in the ability to work together to overcome the obstacles we face. In the aftermath of Pearl Harbor and 9/11, we came together – in DC and all across the country – to stand up for our values and stand against the aggression that took the lives of our families, friends, and coworkers. We can and must do that again...standing up for our neighbor and political opposite.

Look at how Secretary Clinton, Presidents Carter, Clinton, Bush, and Obama came together in solidarity on Inauguration Day. The peaceful transition of power, a core tenet of our democratic institution, meant more than the political differences or personal dislikes between the dignities seated on the dais erected on the U.S. Capitol steps. In fact, with the exception of Donald Trump, all the living American Presidents (Democrats and Republicans) are good friends. All have collaborated on numerous issues during and after their presidencies, reaching across party lines to initiate change and tackle difficult challenges.

We've always believed that the best days of America are ahead of us...now we just need to reach out and take them. It's time to go for gold and restore once again with conviction and humility our presence on the global stage. To release what has held us back and reset what has slowed us down. It is too late to think about yesterday! As President Clinton once said, "Yesterday is yesterday. If we try to recapture it, we will only lose tomorrow." We must concentrate on the future and start driving forward once again, instead of spinning our wheels in a rut, getting bogged down by partisanship, or rolling backward altogether.

Today is the time to focus on the road ahead! Time to think about what we want the future to look like, and how we can build that better tomorrow together! Time to move beyond the vitriolic 2016 elections, consider the fights to come, and determine what role we can play in America's future. So join me on this journey, join me in this fight, and together we can plant the seeds of a bright and prosperous future. After all, only by looking forward, coming together, and working with each other can we **Make America Stronger Together Again.**

Afterward

The 2016 campaign was difficult for Secretary Clinton, her family, and the staff of Hillary for America. It was also hard for the rest of America...or at least those who had supported Clinton or opposed Trump. How Trumpism beat out decency and establishment politics still eludes many of us. We had expected a Democratic victory from the beginning, believing since days after Obama won the 2008 primary that Hillary Clinton would be the party's next nominee and the country's first female president. When that didn't happen, we were shocked. I began piecing together this book in the summer of 2017 as I reexamined the Primary and General Election Debates, looking for clues to just exactly what happened.

As I watched the clips of Democrats and Republicans hashing it out, I felt a visceral feeling of sadness. Both sides had good candidates, many of whom could have been effective presidents, although I had a bias towards Clinton and the Democrats. When I got to the three presidential debates between Clinton and Trump, I nearly lost it. I watched as one candidate took on a bully, maintained poise, professionalism, and composure as he belittled and degraded her. I watched as camera crews panned to Bill Clinton

Afterward

in the audience after Trump suggested that the former president treated women worse than he did. I was appalled. I knew at that moment, that America deserved to hear the truth about what got us here and how we can get past this tumultuous time in our nation's history.

This book outlines the campaign that changed our understanding of American politics in detail. I try to summarize what went wrong in 2016 and the years leading up to the race. Many other works already discuss the Russia-Trump connections – likely collusion – so this book only briefly addresses that broad storyline. Instead, I try to lay out a clear platform for where we must go from here. If we want to get beyond the ridiculousness of the 2016 cycle, we need to come together as a country and actually listen. We need to stop being complacent, accepting what we see without challenging the attempts to destroy our values. We must stand united against intolerance and the continued vilification of those who are different. Most assuredly, we must recognize that we are all in this Great American Experiment together. Diversity is woven deep in the fabric of America. At the end of the day, we're all different; our backgrounds are different and our beliefs are different too. America will work best if we accept all of these differences.

The chapters of this book are intended to encourage you to think about what we've been through together and the vision we all have for America in the future. Chapters 12,13, 14, and 15 are named in honor of the 2008 and 2012 campaigns of Senator McCain, Senator Obama, Governor Romney, and President Obama respectively. Note the number of chapters, that's a special nod to the most vitriolic and unique year in American politics. I hope you have fun finding other "Easter eggs" throughout this

Afterward

text, but most importantly, I hope this book inspires you to get involved and do your part to Make America Stronger Together Again.

Cheers! Gregory

Acknowledgements

I dedicated this book to the people who changed my life, the people who showed me a better way, and the people who inspired me to put words to paper.

Thank you to my mother for being the rock in my early years and a sounding board in my adult life – especially during the frustration of the 2016 election and the days that followed. Thank you, thank you, thank you for your feedback on this project, offering guidance in messaging and editing. You've made a permanent mark on every child you've instructed, every family you've helped, every choir you've directed, and everyone who's heard, seen, and been transformed by your incredible talents. I hope one day I can make you as proud of me as I am of you every single day. You make me laugh at the absurdity of presidential politics and I'm sure without your jokes about 2016, life in the Trump Era would B-Flat!

Thank you to my sister who continues to inspire me, make me laugh, and teach me how to become a better debater. It's definitely a "turrible idea" to mess with a strong woman like you! Although I'll never admit it to your face, you've made me a better man by casting an impressive shadow – an example I'll never live up to.

Acknowledgements

Thank you to my grandparents who were always there for me when I was growing up. You are still with me indefinitely in spirit, and I'll always be indebted to you for your wisdom, encouragement, and unequivocal generosity.

Thank you to Katie and David Godino. I don't have words to describe what you both mean to me. I'm so fortunate to have you as family.

Thank you, Wendell Vaughn, for filling a large void in my life. Being your mentee has meant so much to me. I'll always have a special place in my heart for you and Sharon.

Thank you to President(s)* Bill and Hillary Clinton for providing such a fantastic example to young men, like me, and women all around the world. You've started a movement and now it's up to all of us to pick up the torch and press on. You've given me so much as role models both in politics and in being a person with kindness and gratitude in my heart. Hillary, your strength and stamina are a motivation to never quit and never give up. (*By the publication of this work, perhaps it will be clear who REALLY won in 2016.)

Thank you to President Barack Obama, a phenomenal leader who has encouraged me to roll my sleeves up and fight for change. I am so inspired by your leadership, poise, and class. Our awkward side hug was a highlight of my college life.

Thank you, Michelle Obama, for inspiring Democrats young and old to be our better angels and take the high road. "When they go low, we go high." Words of wisdom to live by.

Thank you, Joe Biden, for being, well...Joe Biden. You are an American treasure, a bit quirky, but a role model for all to look up to. There simply is no one else in American history like you...or

Acknowledgements

who rocks aviators while eating a waffle cone of ice cream like you. Thanks for inspiring me.

Life is hard sometimes, but I'm lucky to have so many fantastic, distinguished role models to look up to. In the darkest hours of America's political nightmare, it's relieving to know some fantastic women and men are standing up for our values, our nation, and our image around the globe. Chris Murphy, Cory Booker, Jay Inslee, Jerry Brown, Kamala Harris, Kirsten Gillibrand, Terry McAuliffe, and Tim Kaine – you are the inspiration for the future of the Democratic Party.

Thank you to my editors, Roger and Patti Cox and Kathleen Raley. I appreciate the hours you spent reading through the book, along with your support and feedback, which was instrumental in the publication of it. Extra appreciation to Kathleen Raley for giving me the tools for success: a strong vocabulary and an exemplar of strength, self-control, and composure. I hope the lexis used in this book is befitting of how fantastic a mentor you have been for me. Unlike some cretins cited in this opuscule, you "know words" and you really do "have the best words"!

A shout out to Jody Howard, Barbara Deal, and those who gave me advice on publishing and marketing this book. I have learned so much from your sophisticated guidance. Thank you to Steve and Kathy Soucy and Lynn Livingston for previewing this text for clarity and intelligibility. A big thank you to all the folks at Ingram.

Thank you to my colleagues, professors, and friends at Northeastern University and Oregon State. I'm so honored to be both a Husky and a Beaver alumnus. Lux, Veritas, Virtus – Go Beavs!

Thank you to my fierce political debaters (you know who you are) and all the people who've challenged me to build a solid case,

Acknowledgements

execute a firm rebuttal, and carry out a political debate. Thanks to you, I've perfected my proficiency to defend my party, political role models, and positions on the issues.

Special thanks to Jennifer P., Emily B., Adam, Kelsey, Kate, Colleen, Simon, Courtney, Joel, Chris, Sheryl, Aaron S., Maddie, Josh, Anna L., Courtney F., Mary T., and Eleanor K.

A final thank you to my many friends, everyone who has helped guild me along life's journey, and everyone who has made an impact on my life.

About the Author

Gregory T. Christensen was born in Palm Springs, California, growing up in the Coachella Valley until his family moved to the Southern Oregon Coast. He graduated from Oregon State University in 2015 with a B.S. in Agricultural Sciences and minors in Geography and Animal Science. He received a Master of Science degree in International Relations and Diplomacy from Northeastern University in Boston with the summa cum laude distinction. The quintessential Democrat, Gregory has worked for a U.S. Senator, worked with a former U.S. President, and has been involved in numerous statewide and national campaigns. A writer, political commentator, strategic community advocate, and citizen diplomat, he spends his time traveling the country, cultivating political conversations on key issues and speaking about foreign affairs and diplomacy to Americans of all stripes.

MAKE AMERICA STRONGER TOGETHER AGAIN
Looking Beyond America's Most Vitriolic Election

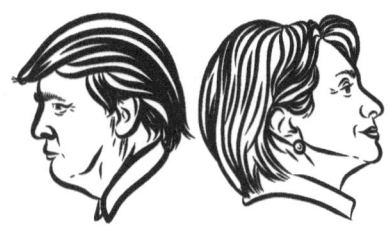

GREGORY T. CHRISTENSEN

AMERICAN BLUEPRINT PUBLISHING

2018

www.ingramcontent.com/pod-product-compliance
Lightning Source LLC
Chambersburg PA
CBHW020402080526
44584CB00014B/1139